Lady *of* Realisation

Lady *of* Realisation

A Spiritual Memoir

Sheila Fugard

BALBOA.
PRESS

A DIVISION OF HAY HOUSE

Also by Sheila Fugard

NOVELS
The Castaways
Rite of Passage
A Revolutionary Woman

POETRY
Threshold
Mythic Things
Reclaiming Desert Places
The Magic Scattering of a Life

Balboa Press books may be ordered through booksellers or by contacting:

Balboa Press
A Division of Hay House
1663 Liberty Drive
Bloomington, IN 47403
www.balboapress.com
1-(877) 407-4847

ISBN: 978-1-4525-4736-7 (e)
ISBN: 978-1-4525-4735-0 (sc)

Printed in the United States of America

Balboa Press rev. date: 8/17/2012

Foreword

Gelongma Khechog Palmo was a pioneer in bringing Tibetan Buddhism to the West. She was known as Freda Bedi, with a degree in political science from Oxford University, who then married a sikh, and fought for Independence in India. She was the first western woman ordained as a nun in the Tibetan Buddhist tradition.

Her life as an Englishwoman in India was extraordinary both as an academic political activist and a social worker. At the request of Nehru, she was chosen to help the Tibetan refugees when China invaded Tibet.

Sister Palmo is remembered today as one of the key figures in bringing the sixteenth Karmapa to America and Europe. She was always at his side, with advice, and reassurance. Her influence was there too with younger important Rinpoches, like Trungpa Rinpoche and Akong Rinpoche, as well as many others. Her work was pioneering, at a time when there were few others to share this task.

Sister Palmo was also a distinguished scholar and translator. She was assisted in this work by the learned lamas of the Kagyu lineage, especially the renowned teacher, Thrangu Rinpoche. Her translations into English bear both an authenticity and rare beauty of language. She is known for her "Garland of Morning Prayers," various sadhanas, and a translation of Mahamudra, known as the "Great Seal," the highest form of meditation.

It was my privilege to have been her student, study, and then travel with her. This memoir is a reflection of that extraordinary time of the arrival of Tibetan Buddhism in the West in the seventies.

This memoir brings with it deep, personal experiences from my own life lived out during the long and brutal years of the apartheid government in South Africa. I was recovering from a breakdown and meeting Sister Palmo changed my life. I encountered not only a Buddhist nun, but also a woman who had marched with Ghandi, been imprisoned, and harassed by the British authorities in India. There were many journeys across oceans that I made to be in her presence.

Sister Palmo reminded me that after the Buddha's passing the teachings were deeply rooted, thrived, and bore fruit. The Dharma, the imprint of the Buddha spread. Ceylon, China, Japan, and Tibet embraced Buddhism, and absorbed the teachings into their own cultures.

She understood the changing needs of society. She spoke eloquently when she said "The words of the Buddha are a balm to soothe soreness...read them. The waters of the Dharma are refreshing...study it. The lotus rank of the Sangha bring forth new flowers...treasure them."

Sister Palmo felt that in America, and other parts of the world, Buddhism still possessed such a relevance. She explained that Buddha exemplified social equality. His wisdom understood suffering as the condition of life. Buddha showed the way to alleviate this. The Way means striving now when the foundations of the world are collapsing. It is a time when familiar customs and ideas are no longer viable. A time when conscience must be ruthlessly examined and racial attitudes changed. The life of the Buddha exemplified the complete freedom. The teachings of the Buddha show the way to enlightenment.

Sister Palmo travelled the world during the seventies on the instructions of His Holiness, the Sixteenth Karmapa. He told her to lead those with little dust on their eyes to the wonder and holiness of the Buddha. She taught profoundly by example, her own radiance being enough to encourage the inward turning of the mind that must set about its own profound enquiry.

Her way was transcendental, and in life she put into practice the great simplicity of a Buddhist nun. All things of the world of material knowledge had fallen away. She had penetrated deep into the nature of suffering, and understood impermanence.

Many were devoted to her as a teacher, guide, and spiritual friend. She was free of her own clingings and viewed all with a deep compassion born of the knowledge of emptiness. Like a good teacher, she taught that each must find their own truth and that the Buddha himself was only a finger pointing the way.

In her mid sixties, failing in health, Sister Palmo was preparing to withdraw from travelling and teaching. His Holiness, the Karmapa, granted her some land in Rumtek Monastery in Sikkim.

A small hermitage was being built there. During the last months when news of the blessing of the land for the hermitage reached me, I had a vision of this magical woman finding a haven.

The hermitage too would be a place where devotees would have joined her to watch a sunset over the Himalayas or listened to the wind brushing the lotuses on the lake. But something other - the need for rebirth for higher work or a place in the paradise of great bliss came sooner than expected. Sister Palmo was gone, rainbows cracked the sky, and the earth was flooded with light.

The life and work of Sister Palmo continues to inspire others on the path. She brought together the ancient yogic tradition of the woman yogis of the past together with insights into contemporary life. Her teachings are invaluable. They open a door into the practice of Buddhism in our everyday journey.

Sheila Fugard, California 2011

Lady *of* Realisation

I did not expect to find you. When I did encounter your presence my life was touched by a magical quality for five years.

You were as rare as the wish-fulfilling gem. The magic jewel of the Buddha's that grants all wishes. The language of Buddhism is decorative. Phrases bear the resonance of an exotic cultural past,"The Precious Minister," "The Wish Granting Tree," and "The Treasure Mountain." A thousand alluring goddesses of unsurpassed beauty exist in the pantheon of Tibetan Buddhism.

You were named Karma Tsultrim Khechog Palmo. The "Karma" signified that you were a pupil of the Tibetan Guru, Gyalwa Karmapa, head of the Kagyu Sect of Tibetan Buddhism. The "Tsultrim" depicted morality. "Khechog" meant knowledge supreme. You were best known by the name "Palmo," the Lady of Realisation.

I recognised you as the Lady of Realisation. You were a Buddhist nun. You gave to my ordinary existence a profound awareness.

1

Friendship and my relationship with you as a spiritual teacher were gifts beyond price. You opened many doors to the Buddhist teachings and opportunities for encounters with high lamas. Beyond all this, there was your radiance that compelled me to make arduous journeys. I travelled from Africa to England, America, and Canada to be in your presence. Yet you were not a person for whom a special relationship could exist. You had taken the renunciation of a Buddhist nun. You were tolerant and open to all.

The aspect of the yogi about you fascinated me. I sensed this power. You were discreet about your attainments. You discouraged speculation about the states of meditation. Yet, there were moments when you seemed intuitively to convey truth: teaching by means of a gesture or unspoken word. You moved in the unfathomable depths of the adept. Yet you remained as seemingly part of this world of phenomena as myself or any other fallible being.

Cape Town and the late summer of 1972- the mountains glisten with a last flush of sustained heat. The place is a secluded house in a quiet suburb. You had arrived from India, and are staying with Rosemary, an elderly devotee whom you had encountered in India ten years ago.

Sister Palmo, you sit cross-legged upon a couch. You are a woman of sixty-one. Shaven head. Clothed in the maroon robe of the Mahayana Buddhist nun. You are a woman stripped to the 'bare essentials.' Grey deep set eyes. Firm bone structure. Your skin, though aging, bears a unique softness. You gesture toward a chair.

There is tranquillity about your bearing of one who has lived many years in the East. Yet, you possess an intellect that is eminently Western. Skills of your early life add to your collectedness.

"Sister Palmo, I have visited many teachers seeking inner stillness... the void...written about in scripture and sutra. Sufi teachers and swamis have offered advice and explanation as regards the nature of mind; meditation, problems of living. None has really helped. The knots of personality remain unresolved."

You see through my spiritual materialism. You sense that I am groping in ignorance. You speak in a soft English accent.

"Mind is radiantly pure. Emptiness, the primordial ground underlies both *samsara* and *nirvana*. Suffering occurs through desire. Meditation can cut through ignorance. Your experience of *samsara* is no different to others who are equally bound by attachment, and thereby incur suffering."

You force me to listen. It is more than the words which you speak. It is your presence. You are a radiant and immaculate example of the Buddha.

"The world of meditation is of extraordinary beauty," you explain. "In mastering concentration and ecstatic vision, all concepts and confusion fall away. There is only a unified and perfect vision. In Samadhi, the radiant Dharmakaya manifests. All is attainable by the pupil. Initiations of the guru, proper instruction, and firm endeavour are necessary."

Sister Palmo, you embody the silence of mountains and the azure sky of summer. Outside, in warm sunlight, I recall your image. The nun in maroon robe, aglow with an agile intellect and profound compassion that awakens a response in me. You have so keenly expressed truth. Buddhist philosophy declares *samsara* and *nirvana* to be one. This is the *koan* which you have now given.

Sister Palmo, you had written letters from Asia. You had been travelling then in Nepal and Thailand. You were usually resident at the Dharma Chakra Monastery in Rumtek, Sikkim, close to your guru the Gyalwa Karmapa. These letters had already prepared me for your arrival. The essence of your personality and that broad understanding of wisdom and compassion had already sustained me during those months when your visit to Africa was only hinted at.

You had written from Nepal. Bounded by Tibet and India, Nepal was at the foothills of the Himalayas. High mountain peaks of Everest and Dhawalagiri arose out of the elevation of Nepal. Strange sounding rivers, the Kurnalli, the Rapti and the Gunuk watered the plains. In the hills, Nepal possessed a climate similar to Southern Europe. More important, Nepal was profoundly connected with the life of the Buddha. This was your reason for a short ten day meditation retreat. You wrote a brief description of this visit in a letter:

....in Nepal, which has all the freshness of an untouched Himalayan country, I had only ten days so chose to spend it quietly in the shrine of Buddhanath, near Kathmandu, known as the Temple of One Thousand Buddhas...

You had travelled in the same year to Thailand. Here in this country, north of Burma and Laos, you spent a quiet stay in a nunnery. Your eyes must have rested upon mangroves, rattans, and the rich rice fields characteristic of Thailand. In the distance, the vast teak forests flourished. Thailand has always been a thriving country. As early as the beginning of the Christian era, trade with India and China was established.

In Bangkok, you had visited the Temple of the Emerald Buddha, an impressive temple in a dark and ornate style. The precious Emerald Buddha is enshrined in a niche high in the wall of the temple. The delicacy of this ancient Buddha moved you to a deep Samadhi. Yet it was the simple life in the Thai nunnery that you wrote about:

A quiet little Upasika Aramaye near Wat Mahadhatu housed me during my fortnight's stay. A second visit. It was almost unbearably hot, and the modern little nunnery, built by the good dayakas of the family Wongsiri Na Ayuthya, had cool laminated floors, electric fans, and a tiled bathroom where we sluiced ourselves with cold water twice a day. The early morning prayers of the Lipasikas led by the head nun, Chantramala, were discreet and beautiful, in Pali and recited in a chant that seemed to mingle with the bird song and silence:

To the Buddha for refuge I go

To the Dharma for refuge I go

To the Sangha for refuge I go

The nuns and their friends could not have been kinder, and the delicacy and variety of food they offered me in traditional style on a circular wicker table amazed me afresh every day.

You embody this background of Asia and the different traditions of Buddhism. In those days, in Cape Town, you are truly at the heart of the ceremonies which you perform. You erect a shrine with tiered candles, flowers, an image of the Buddha, a photograph of the Gyalwa Karmapa, and offerings of fruit and cake. Dominant is the image of Buddha Sakyamuni, in the enlightenment pose. You lead the meditation with a text of the Buddha: Amitabha, the Buddha of Boundless Light, who appears with the red colours of the setting sun.

These ceremonies do not lessen the horror attendant upon Africa. The dark twisted roots of racism continue to proliferate. Rather, Sister Palmo, you bring an insight into indestructibility. You proclaim a doctrine of the Buddha that Communist China sought to eradicate with the invasion of Tibet in 1959. In Tibet, all temples, images, and precious texts have been destroyed. Yet the Chinese invasion was not new to the history of Buddhism. The ancient Buddhist University of Nalanda, a place of learning where erudite *pandits* engaged in debate and philosophic and meditative studies reached a peak, was razed by Islamic invasion in India in the sixth century. Then the light of Dharma had appeared to be extinguished.

Out of the destruction of Tibet, an influx of lamas who had escaped to India travelled to the West and proclaimed the ancient doctrines of the Buddha. It is auspicious that you, Sister Palmo, bring this seed to Africa. Intuitively, I realise this, though I could not find words then. The beauty of your expression, maroon robes flowing, and a voice ringing out the poetic phrases of offering to the Buddha.

"All the *Tathagatas* I praise, with symbols, garlands, saffron water, sacred flowers, the ceremonial canopy, perfect butter lamps and pure incense. To the Buddhas I am making this offering. Ceremonial robes and rare perfumes, a pile of butter and barley flour, as high as a mountain ... all I gather together, clean, pure and holy, and all these precious things I am offering to the Buddhas."

These texts remain with me. They describe the myriad manifestations of form before all dissolves in the void. Images of deities that are beyond separateness, differentiation, and ego. The texts and the deities are as indestructible as the vajra and bell, symbols of wisdom and compassion. I marvel that you, Sister Palmo, perform these ancient ceremonies in Africa.

The new Rumtek Monastery was begun in 1961, the Tibetan year of the female iron ox, on the site of an older sixteenth century Kagyu Monastery. Characteristic landmarks still made this area auspicious. Seven streams and seven hills were in close proximity and high snow capped ranges rose up formidably in the distance. A great river, swollen with power, was a torrent close by. This site was to be the seat of the new Kagyu Monastery of Rumtek. Further land about the monastery in Sikkim was obtained through Pandit Jawaharlal Nehru, then the Indian Prime Minister. Food and free clothing was given by Tibetans who worked on the project. Building operations were soon underway.

The Chinese invasion of Tibet in the late fifties had forced the Karmapa Lama from his historic seat of power in Tsurphu, Tibet. Hostilities worsened despite a peace negotiation made by the Karmapa and the Dalai Lama. Lamas were harassed. Monasteries were ransacked. The Red Brigade was loose. Dharma faced annihilation in Tibet. The Karmapa fled the country. He took with him only his sacred relics, tantric texts, statues, icons, and rare books. A handful of followers escaped with him. The journey to India was dangerous and arduous.

Sister Palmo, you recognised the high teachings inherent in Tibetan Buddhism. You had worked closely with Nehru in establishing centres for Tibetan refugees. Your commitment was immediate. Intimations of the sufferings of a people, a need to preserve this ancient culture, and the Tibetan Buddhist religion. Prophetically too, you had found your guru, the Gyalwa Karmapa. Devotion was alive in you. Meditation, profound enquiry, and the aesthetics of puja entered your life. You took the insubstantiality of the void and understood both aspects of wisdom and compassion. You cut through all the officialdom of red tape. You offered immediate help to the lamas and monks.

The new Rumtek Monastery was completed in 1966. It was at the age of fifty-five that you became known as Sister Karma Kechog Palmo, the first Western Tibetan Buddhist nun. You occupied a room in the monastery close to the four highest *tulkus*. You had done many retreats and moved further in the esoteric study of the Tantra than most Westerners. You had passed beyond the superficialities and ambitions of worldly life. You had chosen the higher realms of the mind, and its pure manifestation.

Then you returned to us. You travelled from the isolated life of Rumtek Monastery to Africa. Now you project slides of the monastery that is your home. It was in Rumtek Monastery that you lived in the heightened atmosphere of authentic religious practice. You celebrated on special days the Rite of Long Life.

You watched the preparation of *mandalas*. You bowed before the rites of the fierce Protector, Mahakala.

In the monastery you absorbed the cultural heritage. Your glance took in a precious statue of the Lord Buddha, a face painted with gold, and hair sprinkled with lapis lazuli. Daily, you passed the great mural of the lineage gurus: Siddha Tilopa, Siddha Naropa, Father Marpa, Milarepa, and Gampopa, executed in the traditional Karma-Khadri style of Eastern Tibet. Intensive meditation, and retreats together with the cultural heritage of Rumtek monastery bore special fruit. You, Sister Palmo, were gifted with the power to transmit spiritual knowledge.

At the foot of the mountains, almost as impressive as those about Rumtek Monastery, I watch slides which reflect the faces of incarnate lamas. Sister Palmo, you talk of each lama with insight and knowledge. Delgo Khyentse Rinpoche, a teacher of the Nyingma- Kargyudpa Line, wears long plaited hair, a broad brimmed hat, and holds ritual implements. Khenpo Thrangu, an eighth incarnation and a former Abbot of Rumtek Monastery, is jovial and poses casually for the photographer. Sabchu Rinpoche, who lives in Nepal, wears an enigmatic expression. The small Dru Pon Rinpoche, age seven, a child *tulku,* presents a serious child's face.

The faces and depth of expression of the incarnate lamas are moving. Then, from a profound depth of silence, a man dressed in a pure gold cloth emerges wrapt in a state of samadhi. This is your own precious guru, the Gyalwa Karmapa. An elusive flash of recognition. Then again you project onto the screen the procession of incarnate lamas, all in maroon robes, religious hats, and holding sacred objects.

Rumtek Monastery and its grandeur does not diminish your other activities. Rather, it was the pinnacle. Compassion too was as part of your nature as wisdom. You pitied the women, nuns, a handful of whom had escaped from the nunneries in Tibet. You wept for them. You felt the need to re-establish the Community in India. You found land. You wrote to us in Africa of the building of the nunnery in Tilokpur, near the cave where the Siddha Naropa had meditated centuries earlier.

The erection of the nunnery was fraught with difficulties. The nuns and yourself lived in grass huts while actually building the structure. Then, the huts were accidentally destroyed by fire. You escaped with your life. But you lost many precious texts in Tibetan, which you had been in the throes of translating into English. Yet you were stoical in the face of great loss. After the fire you wrote about the continued labors at the nunnery. A fragment of this letter remains:

...we must build a stone hall, and a few rooms at least before the summer, and it is now our own.

A year later, you were still laboring under the heat of the Asian summer with rations scarce and fruit virtually unobtainable. You wrote despite deprivation of the further developments at Tilokpur:

Our gonpa...the nunnery...building is something of an odyssey. We are clearing bricks and mud from the floor of the ruined fort on top of the hill. Seems like a mountain. Tibetan and Indian labour with the nuns of all sizes, including me, carrying stones for an hour a day. Our little nuns carry pebbles.

The nunnery at Tilokpur was eventually completed. A small community of both Tibetan and Western nuns reside there. They live the life of renunciates, as they would have done in the great monasteries of Tibet. They receive instruction, meditate, and make retreats. The liberation which they will attain has its seed in your actions. You are a 'karma gatherer,' a being able to influence others by perfect action.

Sister Palmo, you graciously accept Cape hospitality and teach the Dharma strenuously. But you are not blind to events in South Africa. The structures of apartheid are abhorrent. Yet you are no stranger to political injustice. You had been active in political life in India. You still visit Indira Gandhi in Government House in New Delhi. You had been a colleague in the Congress Party. You had then been a follower of Mahatma Gandhi. You had fought for Indian independence. You had even been imprisoned for your political beliefs. You had lived with social injustice a long time.

Later in the context of meditation, you inferred that your prison experience only added to the power of meditation. Meditating then in the dawn hours before the slumbering shapes of the other restless women in prison took shape, you had found peace. Drawing upon this knowledge of silence, you had come to terms more easily with deprivation, overcrowding, and inadequate toilet facilities. This experience had nurtured your insights in later life as a teacher of meditation.

Sensing the predicament of conscience and compassion in South Africa, you say:

"It is always the intellectuals that suffer in any repressive society. But such situations toughen the moral fibre. It is a tenacity at the root of *sila* or morality. Non violence is understood through this experience. Gandhi's teachings on *"ahimsa"* did much to formulate my political commitment in those early years for the struggle for independence in India."

Tea is served. You reveal over cake and biscuits that you are the mother of an Indian film star, Kabir Bedi. Your son is a matinee idol of the Asian film industry. Teenagers from Bombay to Calcutta adulate this athletic and bronzed man. You show photographs...a bearded, Indian costumed hero of some mythic legend leaps and smiles from the stills of a colour film. The face of the actor is stunning.

Later, travelling with you, I learn of the paradoxes of your life. You worry about Kabir and the pressures of the Asian film community at Juhu, Bombay. When the marriage of Kabir and his model wife, Protima, fails you stand by magnificently as a resourceful grandmother. In the last year of your life, you had hoped that your grandchildren would spend time with you at the monastery in Rumtek. Kabir would then be filming in Europe. Protima would be touring the U.S.A. as a member of a dance group with Ravi Shankar. Such was the flexibility of Indian life, that it allowed you to be a grandmother as well as a Buddhist nun.

The enormity of your presence is already a burden. You sit lotus posture, and with the power of discourse, shatter my veneer of composure.

"Leave the Wheel of Existence. You have seen enough of suffering. The facts of being born, bearing illness, growing old, and death are painful. Remember Prince Siddartha! Even he was forced to leave wealth, a wife, and an infant son. Resolve the knot of existence. Cut the roots of desire. Examine your life. See how you are bound to samsara."

Bound on the Wheel of Life! I had been whirled from realms of existence as depicted in the Tibetan Wheel of Life. I had surely possessed the ignorance of the animal state. I had known the suffering of the hell beings. Conflicts had warred in me like the grotesque angers of the quarrelsome gods.

I had known deluded peacefulness similar to the *pretas* who live for aeons. Even these beings sense imminent death finally. Their dress becomes soiled. Garlands of fresh flowers fade. Perspiration breaks forth in the armpits. Evil smells arise from the body. I had observed these realms as psychological states. I possess too the rare human form in which it is possible to hear the words of a Buddha.

The tranquillity of your expression, Sister Palmo, and the manner in which you express truth lead me to the commitment of taking Refuge. The shrine is decked with flowers, incense, candles, and an image of the Buddha. You who are a member of the Sangha of the Buddha and have taken renunciation, are able to give Refuge. You sit in the meditation pose, a prototype of the Buddha, who had taken refuge centuries earlier, and of your guru, the Gyalwa Karmapa. You embody the same truth, the understanding of the ultimate ground of being. I repeat after you, the words of the Refuge Ceremony.

IN THE BUDDHA I TAKE MY REFUGE

Accepting that teaching supreme which is free from craving.

IN THE DHARMA I TAKE MY REFUGE

Regarding it as the most excellent among communities.

IN THE SANGHA I TAKE MY REFUGE

Until my death comes, will you most Venerable
one, take me as your disciple.

Like the Buddha of old and Gyalwa Karmapa, you snap your
fingers. I know at this moment that I have received the ordination
of the Buddha. The energy that rushes down my spine and the
bliss that radiates my being convinces me of the reality of the
experience. You give me the name, Dechen, meaning Great
Bliss.

In giving Refuge, Sister Palmo, you turn my vision in a certain
direction. The goal is liberation. I am set upon a path that will
demand complete openness, and the realisation of wisdom and
compassion. I have made this commitment.

Sister Palmo, you urge me to accompany you on a short retreat. I
am confused, unable to assent, surrender myself further. You leave
for a wooded country area. Appalled at the loss of you, I return
to the house in Cape Town, where I had taken Refuge a day
earlier. I meditate before the familiar shrine, rich with the sense
of your presence. In the corner of the room lies your discarded
robe destined for the laundry. I cannot ignore the symbolism of
that garment. I know that I must follow you.

Next day, I travel across the arid landscape of the Western Cape. Past redolent backwaters, along dusty roads, and approach the distant mountains. This is the first of the many incredible journeys that I am to make in search of you.

At the country retreat you are the energetic teacher. You give teachings that are suitable for sustaining students over long periods without the aid of a lama. You teach aspects of wisdom from the HEART SUTRA, the pinnacle of Buddhist teaching.

The dialect of emptiness. The subject of Buddha's Second Turning of the Wheel of the Law on Vulture Peak.

"...Here, U Sariputra, form is emptiness and the very emptiness is form; emptiness does not differ from form, form does not differ from emptiness; whatever is form, that is emptiness, whatever is emptiness, that is form, the same is true of feelings, perceptions; impulses and consciousness."

How can I not be moved by this sutra, the axis of Buddhist wisdom? Apart from classical teachings, you project the powerful energies of Tantra. You invoke archetypal forms of the ancient Tibetan Buddhist religion. In response, archetypal images of Africa in my own mind mingle with these deities of Tibet.

In a moment of truth, you blind my eyes with a red cloth. Then you remove the covering, so that I, the neophyte, see the world anew. I celebrate my adulthood by casting a flower upon the *mandala*. This is the extraordinary fabric which you throw before me. I must piece the strands together for myself.

In the morning, I experience a return of memories that had been dormant in my life. I see myself again upon the Island of Crete. I had visited the island just before a serious illness. The windmills of the Lasisthi plain, the tavern of Chersonnissos return. I see the Aegean, vivid blue, translucent upon sand. Later, a ship took me to the island of Aegena, where wooded slopes and ancient Temples enthralled me. Images of Corinth flew past. The ancient palace of Phaestos, visited in the heat of August, shudders with the same kinetic energy as the deities of the mandala that you have aroused from my sleeping consciousness. Sister Palmo, you had come to Africa. You had shaken me by the arm and woken me from a deep sleep. As for your image, that of the maroon clad bhikshuni, I cannot put that aside either. I must find you again.

Sister Palmo, you return to India, yet your presence continues to inspire. I create my own shrine. The hours which I spend in meditation are full of distraction. The mind is like a rushing river in full torrent. Thoughts crowd in like a horde of enemies, seeking only to distract. The tranquillity that I seek is elusive, hard to realise.

I walk beside the ocean. The beach is fringed with lilies, reeds, and ornate red hot pokers. Boulders take the weight of a fretted tide. I sense your presence here more than before my shrine. Meditation that is effortless is captured here rather than the tense hours spent in taming the mind according to the practice of *samatha* meditation. I hunger after wisdom. There exists in Zen and Tibetan texts, all the inferred splendour of the void. Gampopa, scholar of the Kagyu order, had written that once one possesses such shunyata there is nothing in the world that is not included in it. The Zen Patriarch, Master Huai Jang, had proclaimed in the Seventh Century in China the following *gatha* subtly describing Voidness:

"The mind-ground holds the (flower) seeds

which sprout when moistened by the rain

The blossom of samadhi is formless

How can it decay or come into being?"

I had written a letter explaining the depths of turbulence in which your visit had plunged me. I felt the need to practice more intensive meditation, study sutra, and scriptural texts. But I lived in Africa, far from lamas. You reply with sympathy. You felt intuitively that *karma* will bring us together again. You had just returned from a visit to Hong Kong. There, you had received a special bhikkhuni ordination of the unbroken line of a Tibetan Indian tradition from a Chinese Abbot, the Ven. Ming Chi of the Chan order. You were the first western woman to receive this ordination in 1,100 years. You received the title of gelongma, which gave you equal status with the monk. Mahayana nuns had always been considered less than their male counterpart, the Gelong. You wrote enthusiastically about this experience:

The visit to Hong Kong was an amazing experience. The first sight of the energetic far east, which is far from our deep yogic India, and Tibet; and yet in certain things very much with us. When I returned to Rumtek...mid August...a great welcome with lots of honorific scarves...after having completed the full bhikkhuni ordination for which His Holiness Karmapa sent me, and there was your letter...

Later, when I encountered you in Scotland, you spoke about this ceremony of the Gelongma ordination. You had first taken the bodhisattava vow, the promise to help all beings attain enlightenment:

"However innumerable beings are, I vow to save them;

However inexhaustible the passions are,
I vow to extinguish them;

However immeasurable the Dharmas are, I vow to master them;

However incomparable the Buddha truth, I vow to attain it."

A lighted stick of incense was implanted in the crown of your head. The incense stick burnt down into the scalp. You felt no pain. You recalled the Buddha Amitabha and entered into a deep *samadhi*. You sent a photograph of yourself participating in this ceremony. You are dressed in a black robe for the occasion. Your face, as always, is translucent. The eyes are farseeing. The impression is of a bride; a woman wedded to an idea of truth far beyond the reach of others.

Months later, Sister Palmo, you arrive in England. During that autumn of 1973, I am visiting London together with my family. I join you at Kham Tibetan House, a meditation centre in Saffron Walden.

You welcome me and I sense the consummate yogi beneath the quiet exterior of the nun. You sit cross legged upon a couch. Texts and letters are open upon a table. Flowers fill the room with fragrance. Incense burns. A fierce deity, the Vajra Yogini, decorates the wall. Tibetan Buddhism in all its totality is embodied in you.

"You are well? You have been meditating so firmly. Such resolution and enquiry is commendable. But give me news of your family and friends in South Africa. Of course, I wrote of my recent visit to Hong Kong, the Bhikkhuni ordination, and that I am now a Gelongma..."

You continue to speak about Kabir, the Asian film industry, grandchildren, and your daughter Gulie, whom has recently become engaged. You speak of your elder son, Ranga, who is the manager of a tea estate. Then you tell me the news that Gyalwa Karmapa is to visit the West the following year.

"You must receive the *darshan*, or holy sight of the guru. He will celebrate the Vajra Crown Ceremony, the compassionate blessing of his lineage. You will experience the Maha Ananda, the great bliss attendant upon such an occasion."

I am awed by such a thought. I cannot believe that exiled in the harsh world of Africa I shall fall within the *mandala* of the Karmapa Lama.

Chimey Rinpoche, a young lama born in the Eastern province of Tibet welcomes you. Chimey Rinpoche has been brought up in the monastery of Benchen in Tibet and was destined to become its abbot. After taking up this high position, Chimey Rinpoche was forced to leave the monastery six months later and flee to India. He led many followers and lay monks to safety. Like so many other lamas whom you had helped as a social worker. Chimey Rinpoche had mastered English under your guidance and now taught Western students. Chimey Rinpoche in his welcoming address referred to you, Sister Palmo, as an emanation of the deity, Green Tara. You modestly accept the compliment. Yet, in those early days when you had founded the Young Lamas Home School you must indeed have seemed a manifestation of Tara, in all her mercy.

In your lectures, you talk of the origins of the Goddess Tara. You explain how Tara had come into being. She had been born from the tear of the eye of Avalokiteshvara, the bodhisattva of compassion. Legend tells how Avalokiteshvara emptied the hell realms and lower states of every suffering being. Satisfied that he had truly alleviated suffering in these realms, Avalokiteshvara returned to his home in Riptola. Again, when Avalokiteshvara looked he saw that the hell realms were immediately filled again. It was as if he had never freed suffering beings in the first place. Avalokiteshvara shed tears for these beings. One tear turned into the form of the Green Tara.

Your stay at Khan Tibet House is a brief two days. You suggest that I join you at Samye Ling, the oldest Tibetan Buddhist Meditation Centre in the West, which is situated in Scotland. I agree and experience joy at this anticipation of further teachings.

The following week, I drive up to Samye Ling together with Rosemary, from Cape Town, and Akong Rinpoche, the abbot of the centre. It had been Akong Rinpoche, who, together with the young Chogyam Trungpa had received an invitation to teach at the Johnston House Contemplative Community in Scotland, a piece of land not far from Dumfries. The wildness and remoteness of the area reminded both lamas of the recently invaded Tibet. Here, they thought something of the contemplation deeply won in seclusion as in the hermitages of Tibet might be wrested from the silence of the Scottish countryside. The offer to take over Johnston House came in April of 1967. The centre, Samye Ling, was named after the great monastery in Tibet founded by the original Tibetan Guru, Padmasambhava; a yogi who came from India, bringing a powerful doctrine to a wild and nomadic people. Meditation flourished at Samye Ling, and it is still a remarkable place for students to take teachings and make retreats.

We arrive at Samye Ling in the early evening. The centre looms as a presence in the darkness of autumn. Sister Palmo, you are in the shrine room. You are celebrating a *puja* to the Green Mother, Tara. I sit behind your maroon clad figure. The sweetness of your voice intones mantras. The lyricism of the text sweeps over me.

"...in the state of illumination of the Acacia forest...awe inspiring is that supremely holy place...eternally merciful, of the colour of emeralds, in woman's form, alluring to the heart, bejewelled always....

Ma! O Dolma, Mother of the Victorious ones

I bow in devotion before you

and sing your praises..."

You are performing *mudras* in association with the deity, Tara. I marvel at the elegant expression of your hands; a meaningful cosmic dance. Later, you tell me that the study of *mudra* is the most esoteric aspect of the Vajrayana.

Early in the morning, the gong calls from the Shrine Room. A five-thirty rising. I walk from my room. Pass through the rain filled dawn, my feet slithering in the mud of the courtyard. The Shrine Room is in darkness. The altar glows by candlelight. The Tibetan monk, Samten, fills the water bowls and lights incense. He then chants a hymn to Avaloktesvara in Tibetan.

Later, Sister Palmo, you give a discourse. You are the powerful lecturer, the graduate in philosophy from Oxford. You had for years studied Buddhist philosophy under diligent teachers such as Khenpo Thrangu Rinpoche, abbot of Rumtek Monastery.

You stress the Four Ordinary Foundations; the enquiry which leads the mind towards a religious attitude. The basic meditations upon karma and impermanence must be investigated before the Vajrayana Path is undertaken. You advise students also to consider the preciousness of this human birth. You remind all of the imminence of death. You teach with a gravity and compassion for the student. The subjects are not dry texts, but universal conditions of life itself.

It is my empty hours spent in meditation in the Shrine Room that are difficult. I struggle with inner conflicts. I cannot face the inevitability of decay. I cannot give up the sense of a permanent ego. Surrender seems impossible. This painful discovery remains hidden. I cannot bear to take these anxieties to you. Yet, you do sense my predicament and the tension that I manifest.

You speak of the radiant nature of the mind, the stainless quality of the Buddha, and the immaculate teachings of the Law. You explain that if only we can remove the veils of ignorance, the immaculate nature of the Universe appears.

I remain unconvinced. I feel that to achieve such tranquillity, you, Sister Palmo, must surely have hard decisions to make. I believe that even you must have found it difficult to take the Renunciation.

"Sister Palmo ..." I begin, with hesitation, "...when you were a wife, a mother, a political figure, and a writer, surely the richness of your life was enough? Why did you put it all aside? How could you renounce the face of a sleeping child? I don't believe that the concept that all life is illusion can be the answer. Does the experience of meditation surpass love, creativity, and friendship?"

You reply, speaking in a profound honesty. "In worldly life, all people suffer; the roots of suffering are in samsara. I was active in lay life, even successful. But in Indian life, there is a natural order of events dating back to the time of the writings of the Upanishads. It is not surprising that a husband and wife both find their own spiritual identities once the rearing of children is past."

I understand this fact to be true. The Upanishads speak of the Four Stages of periods in life. The first period is that of the chaste student. The second period is of the married householder. The third is of the recluse who seeks a forest hermitage. The last period is of the mendicant, or bhikshu, who begs a daily meal and meditates.

You explain further. "I was ordained a nun at the age of fifty-five. Transient pleasures had already fallen away. But the warmth of love and compassion remained. But in a wider context, all sentient beings are deserving of compassion. All compounded things wear out. These problems require deep meditation. You may have to face similar issues in your own life. The path is never an easy one."

I believe your words, Sister Palmo. Your life has been a spiritual journey. I have at last understood something of the pure nature of the Renunciation.

The days pass at Samye Ling in meditation and study under your guidance. You had hoped that Rosemary would accompany you on a short journey through Scotland. But Rosemary must leave unexpectedly for Italy. You ask me to join you in her place. Soon the taxi will take Rosemary to the station and the London bound train. I am awed by the prospect of travelling with you. Your radiance may consume me. I will be reduced to nothing, stripped of ego. Poignantly I sit in the dining room, while a youth plays melancholy notes upon a flute. The taxi rumbles up the drive and Rosemary is gone.

I sleep badly that night. Tension is manifest in my drawn expression. I have accepted your offer of the invitation to travel with you. Sister Palmo, you observe my discomfort and remark:

"You have begun Foundation Practice. Meditation in the Shrine Room has been difficult. Purification is always necessary. The stains of the mind, the dross of *karma*, must be cleansed. There is nothing to fear. With the blessing of the Guru, all appears radiant self nature. I urge you to receive the *darshan* of His Holiness Karmapa, when he visits the West next year."

The visit of the Karmapa seems far in the distant future. I know only the present. I will actually travel with you to the small

Scottish town of Stirling. I am immensely grateful and no longer afraid. Sister Palmo, you are the simplest of people to be with.

We break the journey to Stirling with a visit to Akong Rinpoche at Dumfries. The Rinpoche expresses great happiness at receiving you at his home. He arranges a Tibetan style meal in your honour; meat balls and dumplings; Chinese vegetables; and exotic dessert. The meal, eaten in the Lama's kitchen, is far from the nomadic celebrations once held in Tibet.

Akong Rinpoche acknowledges that you were the compassionate Mother, Tara, who had helped the lamas, when they had fled from Tibet. You had wept to see lamas forced to work in road gangs with other refugees in India. Moved by compassion, you set up "The Young Lamas Home School," at Dalhousie, where Tulkus and lamas could continue their religious training and learn English.

Akong Rinpoche recalled the occasion when, as young men, he and Trungpa Rinpoche had come to the verandah of your house. The lamas, still in their teens, were dressed in robes. They pleaded for assistance. You surrendered completely. You took both lamas into your home and your heart. They were treated as sons. In return, you learn the inner aspects of Tantric practices. Your agile mind saw that the Tantric Teachings far surpassed the slower path of the Hinayana way.

You talk of the young Trungpa when in robes, the light that you had witnessed in the lama's face. Celibacy, you explain, heightens compassion, and the energy to transmit teachings. Bodhicitta, sublimated sexuality is the means of this transmission. In your presence, I am constantly aware of your own vow of celibacy and inner aspect that is blissful.

That evening, we watch on the television the wedding of Princess Anne and Captain Mark Philips. Since your ordination, you have seen no films. You are simply an elderly English woman moved by the pomp and ceremony of the occasion. Memories bound up in images of the Queen Mother, members of the Royal Family, and the beauty of Westminster Abbey moved you to speak of your own English background.

You, Sister Palmo, had been born in Derby, as Freda Houlston, in February 1911. Your father, Francis Houlston, a merchant, died in battle in the First World War. You were brought up by your mother, Nellie Houlston, in the town of Derby. You attended the Parksfields Cedars School there. Going up to Oxford changed your life. You helped a fellow scholar study for the entrance exam to Oxford. You made such progress that you too wrote the entrance exam. You unexpectedly were accepted, while the friend failed. A year of living in France with a French family prepared you somewhat for the experience of Oxford.

You went up to Oxford a provincial girl. You left it four years later as a determined radical thinker who had married a fellow student, an Indian, Baba Bedi. These years were so formative that you were already set upon a path that was characteristic of your future life. Two of the great minds of the century were to visit Oxford and influence you. They were Mahatma Gandhi and Rabindranath Tagore.

Gandhi visited England and Oxford in 1931. You immediately came under the spell of the Mahatma. This was a religious leader who had evolved a humanism that went further than the Marxism or Socialism popular with your generation. The *Ahimsa* that Gandhi propagated was a spiritual path based on "correct insight" of the mind and a "non-violence that aimed at ridding the personality of hate, passion, and prejudice." It was a culmination of Gandhi's reappraisal of Hinduism and the writings of Tolstoy. Later, you came to understand this as an aspect of Buddhist meditation... the mind that is energetic in enquiry, and the practice of morality. In India, during the thirties, you became a *Satyagraha*, one who both believed and demonstrates the "firmness of truth." This was the beginning of your long struggle for Indian Independence.

At Oxford you fell in love. The man was a fellow Indian student, Babajie Bedi, a direct descendent of Guru Nanak, a founder of the Sikh religion. You loved Babajie Bedi and shocked your contemporaries by marrying an Asian. Your need to break with conservatism was strong. It had begun with your decision to leave the Anglican Church at the age of seventeen and become a free thinker. Your union with Babajie Bedi, an Oxford Blue, was your first commitment to India; the land that would claim you.

You followed Gandhi, and were attached to the Socialist leader and disciple of the Mahatma, Jayprakash Narayan. You were in those days of political involvement, a professor of English at Fateh Chand College in Lahore. The violence that occurred later before Indian Independence shocked you. It also gave you insight into political change. You understood this during your visit to South Africa in 1972. You sensed that apartheid, like all intolerable systems, would ultimately fail.

Rabindranath Tagore, the ageing and bearded prophet came to Oxford. He was, in contrast to the austere Gandhi, flamboyant and radiant. Tagore spoke about the power of poetry, of an age of spiritual revolution. Tagore had come as an emissary to the West long before the later influx of gurus and teachers: Dr. Diasetz, T. Suzuki, Krishnamurti, Hindu swamis, Zen roshis and lamas. Tagore threw a gorgeous fabric before you; the images of the country which you would soon visit, India. You would travel there with your husband Babajie Bedi. You would leave Derby, the last vestiges of provincialism, and find fulfillment.

Tagore loved and respected Buddhism. He had written a play, called "Worship of the Dancing Girl." Tagore had explored Buddhist legend. The play concerns Nati, a dancing girl, commanded by the King that she should dance before the sacred altar of the Buddha in order to desecrate it. Instead Nati dances a series of *mudras* of devotion. One by one, all the gorgeous wrappings of the dancing girl are put aside as she disrobes during the dance. Finally, Nati is left only in the ochre robe of the nun. Similarly, the outward trappings of your life, Sister Palmo, fell away. Like the dancing girl, Nati, you too are revealed in your essential nature of the nun.

Gandhi and Tagore both influence you at Oxford. Both minds were totally immersed in the new spirit of the age. Tagore was a man of poetry, who believed in the new humanity. Gandhi believed in the same humanity, but saw it transformed through action. You followed Gandhi through the long political struggle. When Indian Independence came you were exhausted. A spark had gone out with the assassination of Gandhi and his cremation on the Ganges. You declined to enter Parliament as a minister. You renounced political life. Instead, you chose to work for the reconstruction of India. You strove to build something new from the ruins of British Imperialism. You turned to social work.

Tagore, you kept in your heart. In your own life you realised the essential vision of Nati, the dancing girl.

India possessed you. Like the Buddha, you had traversed all the holy places: the Four Sacred Shrines...Lumbini, the birthplace of the Buddha in Nepal; Buddhagaya, where the Buddha had attained enlightenment; Varanasi, the place where the Buddha had preached his first sermon to the five enlightened ascetics; and Kusinara, the place where the Buddha had passed into *Parinirvana* in Uttar Pradesh.

You recounted all of this at Akong Rinpoche's home in Dumfries as the images of Princess Anne and Captain Mark Philips faded on the television screen. You are that remarkable combination ...a Westerner, who is also deeply Oriental, yet so subtly blended that it is impossible to sense any line of demarcation.

The train leaves Dumfries. We travel to Stirling, home of your niece, Mary. Ancient stone walls, rolling grass lands, and a cloud filled sky are in view. On the journey through Scotland, I am released from taking teachings within the confines of a meditation centre. I sense the person beneath the robe.

You explain that you had been both a politician and a Professor of English. Yet, you do not elaborate either on literature or politics. Your appetite for knowledge has fallen away. This had happened in India when you had first gone up into the mountains to meditate. Since then, you have not kept up with the flood of information over the past decade. Meditation, Buddhist philosophy, and the encounter with others in the religious sense is your prime concern.

At Stirling, your niece meets us at the station. You embrace this young Englishwoman and her small child with customary warmth. You are her aunt; the magical visitor from India. You have that mistique of the Victorian era, of relatives returning from the East, who become magnified, even exotic, in the minds of others. Yet, you are profoundly conscious of your English roots. Your brother, the father of Mary, was a submarine commander in the Second World War. He had been torpedoed off the coast of India. He had survived many hours in the water.

After his rescue at sea, he had been re-united with you in India. Apart from this encounter, you had been cut off from your English relatives for years. It was only now that during your travels as a meditation teacher that you were returned to your niece in Stirling, daughter of an old aunt still living in the Lake district. Your mother, Nellie Houlston, had already died; your brother too had collapsed after a coronary. It is hard for Mary, your niece, to understand that you had grown up in her familiar England. Your many years in India have altered you. You are a person infused by other cultures, different conduits of information, and unique in being the Westerner who is also genuinely of the East as well.

Responding to your niece's curiosity, and my own unspoken questions, you talk of the central experience of your life. This is your conversion to Buddhism that occurred in Burma. You had always been inclined to contemplation. In your school days, from the age of fourteen, you had meditated in the Anglican Church in Derby. Throughout your married life you had found a period of solitude each day. Hinduism flourished about you in temples, works of art, the Indian way of life, and the *yogis* and *sadhus*. The Sikh religion was strong too, directly influenced by your husband, Babajie Bedi. Yet, none of this satisfied you. You read extensively into Christian and Sufi mysticism. Theresa of Avila, St. John of the Cross, and the poems of Rumi moved you. Buddhism, once strong in India at the time of the great Nalanda University, had been destroyed by Islamic invasion centuries past. There were few books available at that time, either on the life of Buddha, or the practice of Buddhist oriented meditation.

You had reached the age of forty-three with your political career already behind you. As a social worker, an opportunity arose for you to join a United Nations mission to Burma. You arrived at Rangoon, a country where Buddhism, in its present form, survives. You wandered through the Golden Kioung monastery at Mandalay. The architecture, people, and a subtle atmosphere of Buddhism impress you. You viewed the great river, the Irrawaddy. You moved into the interior of rugged hills and encountered crude peasants and artisans. You stood on the edge of vast forests with teak trees sometimes growing to a height of 120 feet. But more important, in Burma, you found a teacher of meditation. There was a monk who was prepared to instruct you. It was no easy task. Westerners did not learn meditation in those days of the early fifties. You had a struggle with the initial lessons. Later, when the Venerable Sayada U Thittilla Aggamahpandita taught you personally, you truly understood the nature of meditation. The Burmese monk gave you a warning. Even after initial instruction, a student often underwent an experience. This experience was not confined to the hours of sitting practice. It could and did often happen in life itself.

Sister Palmo, you left for the hills on field work. Here, the experience about which the monk had warned happened. A vision of a radiant lotus floating upon the sea appeared before you. It was an experience of mystical intensity. Tears had poured down

31

your face. The experience lasted several hours. The mechanical aspects of behavior still functioned. You continued to speak to peasant women; and made observations on agricultural problems. Your fellow social workers sensed that you were elsewhere. They left you alone. Later, your associates gently assisted you to the village sleeping quarters. You had found the essence of what you had sought over the years; the transcendental experience, the unitive wisdom. The solitary hours spent in the Anglican Cathedral in Derby had been the beginning. Those early hours of first light in prison had continued the pattern of meditation. Moments too, in married life, when you had broken away from the physical embrace to a moment of interior silence. You had realised the ultimate bliss. You were like those precious gurus of Tibetan mythology who are born in the heart of a lotus. Miraculous, such beings nurture humanity.

The United Nations project came to an end. You returned home to India. You told Babajie Bedi of the experience. You implied that you could no longer be a wife in the physical sense. The vision of the lotus had cauterised, even burnt away that aspect of your nature. You were now a *bramacariya*, one who has renounced sexual life. But you remained as mistress of your home and mother to your children. India had for centuries seen men and women live in chastity together in the home.

As a Buddhist in India, you were isolated from your teacher, the Venerable U Thittila Aggamahpandita, in Burma; a condition which was worsened when that country was closed for foreigners. You diligently practised the Hinayana Path. But it was not easy to practice over the years without the closeness of a teacher- so necessary for progress on the path.

Apa Pant, the Indian diplomat and a colleague of your political days, urged you to visit the Gyalwa Karmapa, head of the Kagyu sect of Tibetan Buddhism. The Gyalwa Karmapa had only recently arrived in India after fleeing from Tibet. Apa Pant had already been influenced by Tibetan Buddhism and had visited the great Tantric monasteries of Samye, Ganden, Sera and Drepung in Tibet itself.

The encounter with the Karmapa was as unexpected as the experience in Burma. You, Sister Palmo, then a deeply meditative woman of the Hinayana tradition came humbly to meet a regal head of a sect of Tibetan Buddhism. The Karmapa, with warmth, compassion, and a mind plunged in a constant *samadhi*, greeted you. The meeting was veiled by intimations of grace waves. The East abounds in stories of those who, after years of searching, suddenly encounter the being- the saint incarnate in flesh who is oceanic in the power to ripen others. You knew immediately that this Tibetan Yogi was your guru. You, who had wandered so long, had now arrived home. You understood by *mudra*; the manner in which the hand gestures of the Karmapa moved across the crystal *mala*. This was a mind to mind teaching. Words and philosophic dialect were unnecessary. A radiance such as that which you had known in Burma was born in you again.

The Karmapa, on his part, had recognized a relationship with you over lifetimes. He immediately accepted you as a personal pupil. He initiated you and prepared you for the Tantric path. You subsequently made many retreats upon tutelary deities of the Kagyu sect. You developed the profound sense of *bodhicitta;* the inexpressible clear mind realisation of the Buddhas.

You recall both the encounter in Burma and your meeting with the Gyalwa Karmapa to your niece and myself as we sit in the living room of the house in Stirling. You teach not only from a highly disciplined training of the Hinayana vehicle, but draw inspiration secretly from the visionary experience of Burma. In Stirling, I know your kindness as a meditation teacher. I labour with the details of the Tibetan Chakra system and the complex visualisations of the tutelary deity of the mandala. You explain that through this intense path of form, the visualisation of the self as a deity- an inner transformation takes place. The pure and radiant mind emerges. You insist that I must find my own way, develop my own insights. Your knowledge remains mysteriously your own.

The Scottish November night is cold. Your niece makes me a bed on a sofa in the living room. You are distressed. You insist on lending me the outer portion of your robe for warmth. It is the same robe that I had once seen abandoned to the laundry in Cape Town. That robe had urged me to follow you to the mountain retreat in South Africa. Wrapped in this same robe, before sleep, I believe that I shall find you. Distant countries and the isolation of your month long retreats can never cut you off.

Before sleep, I recall events of the life of the Buddha; Gautama, the prince, had left the palace after witnessing the Four Signs... illness, old age, death, and a robed mendicant. The prince had cut off his long hair and donned the yellow robe of the mendicant. He became an ascetic and practiced meditation and austerities.

Driven to despair at failing to find truth, the haggard prince, an emanation of privation, chose a spot beneath a Bodhi tree. He was determined not to rise from this chosen place until enlightenment had been reached. Forces of the unconscious assailed the royal mendicant. But Gautama crossed the barriers of ignorance and the defilements inherent in human nature. The prince of the Sakya Clan, with a superhuman effort, abandoned all familiar territory of habitual mental processes and won through to the state of enlightenment. He had severed the roots of desire. Karma and all its entanglements were cut. There was no more re-birth. Buddha was the *muni*, the one who had gone, utterly gone beyond.

The form of the Golden Buddha fills my dreams as I sleep beneath your robe. I stand on the thresholds of the places of meditation of the Buddha; mouths of caves; shade under the great Pepul tree; beside flowing streams.

At breakfast I return the maroon outer robe to you, Sister Palmo, the rightful owner. The robe is your daily attire. A garment that is rough, worn, and travel stained. It is essentially you, the *bhikshuni*, the intimations of Buddhahood hidden in the cloth.

The stay in Scotland is over. For me, it has been a time to get to know you as a person. But the power of the woman to move me in no way erases my powerful initial impression of the yogi. A farewell to your niece in Stirling. Then, a brief visit to Glasgow. Then homeward bound for us both on the Glasgow-London express.

As you prepare for sleep, you notice that I am restless and wide awake. You gently explain to me something about the yoga of dreams as practised in Tibetan Buddhism.

"The Yoga of dreams is a method of entering the dream state and exploring it without waking. In this manner, the adept sees that dreams are as illusory as reality experienced when awake. Both states will be seen to be identical. This teaching is part of the Six Yogas of Naropa. But it is a fairly advanced teaching. The foundation practice must be completed first, before the study of the Six Yogas is undertaken."

At Euston station, we drink early morning coffee on arrival. You are no longer the adept or the teacher of philosophy, making clear the essence of your study over the years with Khenpo Thrangu Rinpoche at Rumtek Monastery. Rather, you are an elderly woman who has made a long overnight journey. The pallor of your face and the lines of exhaustion about the eyes remind me again of your frailty. Swiftly, I hire a taxi to take you to Indian relatives in Hampstead. They will have a comfortable room prepared for you on arrival. Travelling as your companion has enriched me beyond measure.

Next day, I am in your presence. You are refreshed after the long journey. In the house in Hampstead, you are surrounded by flowers, fruit, and incense. You suggest the insubstantial quality of Tara, the mother of compassion, in your gentle bearing. You observe that the dark forces of the unconscious that had threatened me at Samye Ling have been dispelled. You convince me that these forces can become transformed into creative energy. You then explain that you must leave shortly for India. The visit to England and Europe is over. You bless me formally. I know that soon you will be again at the Dharma Chakra Centre in Rumtek. You will be surrounded by distant snow-capped mountains, and the green rice valleys. It does not worry me that you will be far away. This is your place in time and space. There is the certainty of seeing you again. The Karmapa will be coming to the West, the following year. You will be close to him, traveling in his party and assisting. There is the assurance of the continuity of the teachings. It cannot be otherwise. You are the Lady of Realisation.

At the end of February I return to Africa. In the cottage above the Indian Ocean, I meditate before the shrine of reeds, shells, and a Buddha Rupa. My life settles down to caring for a family and writing. Your presence, Sister Palmo, is powerfully alive.

In a letter from Sikkim, later in the year, you inform me of the impending departure of the Karmapa and his party to the west. You are most certainly included in that auspicious group. I decide to join you in America.

I leave Johannesburg on a raw spring day. I arrive in New York in a blaze of autumn colour. I recall images of you, Sister Palmo, during my long flight; the nun in the silent house in Cape Town; the friend who lent me the bhikshuni's robe in Scotland; the elderly woman pale with fatigue after the rushing night train journey.

I join you in San Francisco and check into a hotel in Berkeley. Barbara, your American devotee, gives me news of an initiation which the Karmapa will bestow the following morning. You insist that I attend the ceremony and receive the blessings and empowerment of the Kagyu lineage. I know only my good fortune to be in California during this auspicious visit.

Next morning, I take a cab to an address in Berkeley where the initiation will be given. Zen students, Hindu devotees, and students of Trungpa Rinpoche wait respectfully for the arrival of the Karmapa. At last, the Karmapa Lama appears dressed in the maroon robe of the gelong. He is leaning upon the arm of Trungpa Rinpoche, who is dressed in the yellow robe. Both lamas enter the hall, followed by the monks.

The signal is given for us to file into the hall. All are neophytes, and sit cross legged upon the floor. The Karmapa Lama is enthroned upon a golden dais. He is the Vajra Master, surrounded by ritual implements. We, the neophytes hold rice, a stick of incense, or a flower as an offering. The Karmapa chants the refuge and *bodhisattva* vows. The invocation of the Universe follows, and the world is seen as the mandala of the guru. Specific deities are invoked. The empowerment is then bestowed upon those present. The spontaneity of *Mahamudra*: the highest non dual meditation is the seed of this empowerment. Finally, the Karmapa shares the merit with all sentient beings.

The beauty of this moment, the Karmapa's *mudras*, and the chanting of the monks cannot overshadow your precious form, Sister Palmo, silently in the background. Yet, so irrevocably part of this spiritual event.

After the initiation ceremony, I find you in the crowd. Sister Palmo, you emerge from a crowd of disciples and embrace me with customary warmth:

"I'm so glad that you managed to come to San Francisco. It is a great blessing to receive an initiation from His Holiness, Karmapa. But you must receive an audience with His Holiness as well. Come with me let me take you to him."

Students of Trungpa Rinpoche drive us to the solid and impressive American style house in San Francisco where the Karmapa and monks are housed. Good as your promise, you insist that I be presented to the Karmapa together with the American poets. You are always conscious that I am a poet of Africa. Allen Ginsberg, Lawrence Ferlinghetti, and Michael McClure are among the poets waiting to be received in audience by the Karmapa.

Together, with Allen Ginsberg, I bow before the Karmapa. Without the dorje and bell, symbols of the Vajra Master, the Karmapa is a man of simplicity. Michael McClure, the West Coast poet, presents the Karmapa with a delicate miniature of a bird in a glass case. The Karmapa holds up the case enclosing the bird as if invoking it to find wings and fly. The intense gaze of the Karmapa possesses all the mystery of a great siddha.

Allen Ginsberg, with a full black beard, and gentle hands, addresses the Karmapa:

"Does His Holiness recall my visit to Rumtek some years ago? Then I had asked you whether the taking of LSD was a valid spiritual path."

The Karmapa smiles, and shakes his head, and replies, through an interpreter:

"The use of drugs creates an artificial sense of higher consciousness. Only mind in its natural state, a complete openness, the practice of *mahamudra* achieves this."

There is laughter in response to Allen Ginsberg's question from the other beat poets; those who had progressed through the exploration of consciousness in the sixties. Lawrence Ferlinghetti sits in silence, like another Mahakashyo, the disciple of Buddha who received a direct transmission by simply witnessing a gold flower in the hand of the Blessed One.

Aware of Africa, a world of harsh sunlight and rugged terrain, I ask the Karmapa for predictions of that land. This Guru, who had witnessed Tsurphu overrun by the Red Guard, replies:

"Suffering is inherent in life. Buddha is the remedy for suffering. Know that at some time the consciousness of a Buddha will awaken in Africa."

The audience is over and the Karmapa smiles a farewell blessing. We respectfully file out of the room. So much has passed through my mind that I am silent before you, Sister Palmo.

You gently insist that I return to my hotel. A young poet gives me a lift across the bridges that link San Francisco with Berkeley. In the quiet room at the hotel I meditate upon so much that has happened. All this experience has the texture of a myth with strands that link Asia, Africa, and America.

The Karmapa performs the Black Crown Ceremony at Fort Mason. Throughout history, it has been the function of each Karmapa to perform this ceremony for the sake of all sentient beings. Whoever witnesses this ceremony will never again take rebirth in the realms of suffering. The fifth Karmapa, Teshin Shegpa, first wore the present Vajra Crown in the Fifteenth Century. This is the crown which is now in the possession of the present Gyalwa Karmapa. When Teshin Shegpa visited China the Emperor Yung-Lo, a devout disciple, saw an invisible crown hovering above the head of Teshin Shegpa. Emperor Yung-Lo had a physical replica made of the miraculous crown which he had seen in a vision. The crown is still said to have the power of transmitting enlightenment on sight.

A throng of two thousand people from San Francisco fill the Fort Mason area. Again, the beautiful people come, with flowing robes, flowers, Indian shirts, colourful saris, long hair, and beads. All have come for the great blessing of the Vajra Crown Ceremony.

The stage is set for the Ceremony as monks sound the Tibetan horns. It is like a scene from a medieval pageant. The Karmapa mounts the dais. The monks bow and present the precious box containing the heirloom, the Vajra crown. (A monk wears a cloth about his face so that his breath will not disturb the ancient fabric.) The crown is placed upon the Karmapa's head. The Karmapa pronounced a *mantra: OM MANI PADME HUNG.* The Karmapa enters a deep *samadhi.* He has assumed the attributes of Chenrezi, the Bodhisattva of compassion. A great energy of compassion fills the arena. The concentration of the crowd reaches a breaking point. Then as mysteriously as it had arisen, the tension is gone. Your face, Sister Palmo, watching this yogic feat, authenticates the veracity of my experience. The Karmapa, all smiles, blesses each individual with a precious relic from Tibet.

As I leave Fort Mason, I wonder how such a guru, the Karmapa, comes to pass like an ordinary person in American society. Comprehending the needs of the divided psyche of Western man, this guru has come to America bringing gifts such as the Vajra Crown Ceremony. The yogi, whom I had witnessed in deep samadhi an hour ago, is also a skilled diplomat and friend who mingles with ordinary Americans in parks, museums, and homes.

There is a reception for the Karmapa at a Japanese hotel. Then we go to an old house in San Francisco, on Capp Street, the home of Tamara Wasserman. The house is tastefully furnished. Thangkas frame the walls and butterflies are preserved under glass. You rest on a sofa. I remain sitting cross legged upon a cushion on the floor. As you sleep, I sense the areas of your life which I can never penetrate; the yogi; the renunciation; your relationship with the Gyalwa Karmapa. These facts remain closed, unspoken even. You are deeply mysterious as a person, despite the outward simplicity of the Buddhist nun. Your profile in sleep has a softness. Wisdom emanates from your form like an ancient stone Buddha from the temples of Ceylon. You wake slowly like an insect fluttering from a cocoon into a world of light. We drink tea in Tamara's kitchen. A breeze comes off the Pacific Ocean. Later, you give teachings to those that come...Jose and Miriam Arguelles, Tamara, and others. You speak of the miraculous nature of the mind:

"Mind in its natural state is radiantly void. The sense of a permanent ego dims this inner light. The initiations and blessing which His Holiness Karmapa is giving purify the dross of ego. *Abhisheka* also means to wash, to purify. Through initiation, the vehicle of the body is made pure. The higher energies can be channelled into states of meditation. If there is effort, struggle with fundamentals such as kindness and generosity; then one is very much at the beginning of the path. Once the activity of the Bodhisattva energy begins to be activated the flow of energy becomes subtle, direct, and increasing. But at the beginning, there is the need for purification and the blessing of the guru."

After the discourse, you bless upon the head with a text of the words of the Buddha. Again, I travel across the bridges that link San Francisco to Berkeley. I re-examine the truth about which you had spoken. Images of the initiation and the great humanity of the Karmapa move me to assimilate the truths about which you have expounded. Like a thief, I enter my own room at the hotel. I am divorced from my clothing, personal possessions, and books. They no longer appear to belong to me. Your presence, Sister Palmo, has freed me briefly from my own sense of ego.

In the Shrine Room of the Nyingmapa Centre in Berkeley, the ancient school of Tibetan Buddhism established by Padmasambhava, the Karmapa bestows the Buddhist precepts. Before the ceremony, Sister Palmo, you comment on the necessity of taking the precepts:

"Precepts are rooted in the Hinayana tradition. They are the basic moral teachings of the Buddha. Precepts invite us to be true to ourselves. The first three precepts are concerned with killing, lying, and stealing. The following two forbid adultery and the taking of liquor and drugs. Precepts form the basis of Dharma."

The Karmapa graciously conducts the ceremony. Twelve of us, a mere handful who had attended the Crown Ceremony at Fort Mason, are the recipients of the blessing. You give explanations throughout the ceremony, and finally say:

"His Holiness exhorts you to be happy. This is a joyous occasion. Morality is the basis of freedom."

In the garden of the Nyingmapa Centre, you elaborate further on the implications of the Buddhist precepts:

"We are all old warriors, who have lived many life times. We have inhabited the world of animals, fighting and quarreling, living only for the moment. We have passed into the state of hell beings and the hungry ghosts suffering unremitting pangs of remorse. We have lived in the higher states of the gods suffused in happiness. But even this joy has been incomplete.

Always we have been forced to take re-birth again and again. In this life, we have found a precious human body and a mind capable of receiving the Buddha's teachings. Precepts held up create wholesome karma. They are the foundation of holistic living. They create a unity within the personality. We are no longer in conflict with the self. A calm mind naturally arises."

You give this discourse with the Pacific Ocean a distant rumble. Your words echo from the past; they are ancient. The core of these Teachings was propagated by Lord Buddha centuries earlier.

Sister Palmo, you are a rich presence in the San Mateo garden. You are at peace beside the stone Buddha at the rockery. Barbara, a close devotee, is the decorator and landscape gardener. A hidden premonition prepared her to take trouble over the years with the house and garden knowing that you, the Lady of Realisation, would live and teach here. You emanate great happiness. The Karmapa has been warmly received in America. Many have received the blessing of the precious guru. You are fulfilled. In the garden I recall aspects of your life.

You surely possessed this same radiance when you had entertained princes and politicians in your Kashmir home. The saris, which you had worn, flowers in your hair, and the glamour which you had possessed, were all put aside. You had perceived an elusive vision which was hard to realise. You understood the truth underlying reality. You understood that the constructions people place upon events and circumstances is born of ignorance. Reality, truly observed, is devoid of association. Existence, purified of emotional attitudes, is radiantly pure.

You withdrew from the world. You took the ordination of a Buddhist nun. From that moment onwards you dressed in a robe. Unresolved conflicts, disturbing emotions, and ignorance were severed through meditation. Until your sixtieth birthday, you were cut off, meditating in the mountains, exploring the shoals of the mind. You reached a resolution, a conviction best interpreted as *bodhicitta*, the enlightened motivation to help others. Having understood profound mysteries, you could lead others to the source.

There are moments in the garden at San Mateo when I sense the past. The writers shine through clearly in the texts of beauty which you have translated into English from the original Tibetan. The social worker emerges in the practical assistance you give to the young. Nothing deters you. Problems of drugs, sex, and alienation are understood. The Buddha is the remedy for suffering. I never think of you as old. You are timeless, accessible, and deeply intuitive. You have in those years of retreat at Rumtek monastery come to terms with impermanence, sense of a permanent ego, and death. These subjects, the classical meditation of the Buddha, are not dry and remote. You make them facts of life for all to study.

You understand meditation. You have travelled the path from concentration and insight to *Samadhi*. You have completed the stages of Mahamudra meditation. The subtle insights bestowed by deities such as the Green Tara and the Vajra Yogini are secret to you alone.

Yet you are more than a teacher of meditation. You are a symbol of renewal. I know that by your act of returning from the mountains that you believe in humanity. Somehow goodness can prevail. The energy crisis, pollution, and terrorism are only the familiar furies of history appearing in new guises. You have progressed beyond these painful dualities. You propound a realisation beyond good and evil. You learnt that during those years of retreat at Rumtek Monastery. This is the reason why you have come back. You, Sister Palmo, are marvelously intact. You represent the indestructibility of the pure mind. With you gone, I recall this valour in all its immaculate purity. I seek it, relentless, in my own nature.

In the morning you are on the way to Vancouver together with the Karmapa and monks. I gave you a promise that I would meet you in Toronto soon. The following day, roaring engines take me back to Kennedy airport. My strands of *karma* with you, Lady of Realisation, are already intermingled. Another pattern is emerging. A few short weeks and I will be again re-united with you, Sister Palmo.

Some weeks later, arriving at dusk at Toronto airport, I take a cab to Bodhisattva House, a Buddhist centre. You had left a message there telling me that you had gone ahead to Bellville where a Tibetan settlement had invited the Karmapa to perform the Vajra Crown Ceremony. You suggest that I join you there. A group of young Tibetans give me a lift to Bellville. These Asian teenagers, now settled in Canada, have adopted a Western lifestyle. Like nominal Catholics, they know only the outward trappings of Tibetan Buddhism. They invoke the Bodhisattva, Chenrezi, and show respect to the Dalai Lama and the Karmapa. But they look with humour at me attempting to meditate seriously.

At Bellville I find you staying at a motel together with the Karmapa and party of monks. You simply accept that I have arrived safely. Sometimes I imagine that you and the Karmapa are like a magic show that might simply vanish into thin air! Yet here in this comfortable motel, you are flesh and substantiality. You have been reading the books of Carlos Castenada. You comment that the lore of the Indian sorcerer, Don Juan, can be interpreted in the Tibetan esoteric teachings. You compare the power of Don Juan to the Tibetan adepts able to create *tulpas*, a projected thought form which takes the human shape. These *tulpas* can be created and dissolved at will. You point out that the energy of a *tulpa* can become dangerous if the adept is not the complete master of his own projection. The idea of the *tulpa* is the same as the Western concept of the "doppelganger," the replica of the real person. You insist that you have to keep up with some reading in order to answer the questions put to you by young Americans.

I bring a small Buddha *rupa*, a genuine Tibetan artifact that bears the authentic seal of origin for the Karmapa to bless. You immediately arrange an audience. You usher me into the presence of the guru. The Karmapa rests in a comfortable chair. I present a white scarf and prostrate three times; the customary protocol before the head of a Tibetan sect of Buddhism.

The Karmapa, face wreathed in smiles, breathes life into the Buddha rupa. Quite simply, I know that I have come as a Westerner, as naturally to this great guru as any peasant had come centuries earlier to an ancient Karmapa in the past of Tibet.

In the morning, a slow train takes us to Montreal. You sit in the lotus posture on the train seat. I make you comfortable with a blanket and pillows. Turning from the bleak landscape, I question you about meditation. You speak of the arising of the *bodhicitta*, the enlightened processes of the Six Yogas of Naropa. I sense your power as an adept.

Mike and Ebba Breacher meet us at the Montreal station. You had met them on their honeymoon in Kashmir over twenty years ago. You had been Freda Bedi then, and it was shortly before you had gone to Burma and embraced Buddhism. They show no surprise at the robe, shaven head, and spare profile. You are still Freda, the magical woman of Kashmir. Mike and Ebba sense your preciousness. You had been a good omen on their honeymoon Then Mike had been a colleague, a lecturer in political science in Fateh Chand College in Srinagar. Ebba, new to India, and imbued with a fierce Hebraic quality had thrived on her friendship with you.

In the Montreal apartment, you recall life in India. You speak of Pandit Nehru. Your children had called this statesman "Uncle" and Indira Gandhi, his daughter, was your comrade in the political struggle. Somehow the robe which you now wear fails to obscure the woman whom you had once been. Freda Bedi is never diminished by Sister Palmo. Freda had travelled across India, made speeches from political platforms, inspiring women of all classes...untouchables, peasants, and illiterates. Sister Palmo has travelled across Europe, Africa, and America bringing a different message of hope.

There is an ease in which you have returned to Mike and Ebba Breacher though years have passed. You are again that mysterious traveller who has made the journey to the East. You have returned with a treasure; the innate purity of your own nature and a mind that shines with such a radiance that reflects those images of political and academic life in Kashmir, yet remains silent at the centre. Here in the company of old friends, you revisit the past. Images of marriage, children, Nehru's profile, the deprivation of weeks in prison, appear before you. Others might have found these memories drenched with emotion. Through your mastery of Mahamudra meditation, such images are seen as radiantly empty. They appear as phantoms of the past.

You, Sister Palmo, acknowledge and recognise your old life. Yet, it has no power to move you to regret or sorrow. You had come up to Oxford a provincial English girl. There, you had encountered Gandhi and Tagore. A handsome Sikh, Babaji Bedi, had claimed you and brought you to India as his wife. In middle life you saw political strife and encountered spirituality in Burma. Later, you became the pupil of the Gyalwa Karmapa and finally took the renunciation of the Buddhist nun, bearing the name Karma Khechog Palmo. All are different textures of experience. The veils have been removed one by one, like Tagore's dancing girl, Nati. Now, you wear the final garment, the maroon robe of the Bhikshuni.

Returning to Toronto, you are anxious to attend an Ecumenical Congress which is being held in the city. Catholic and Protestant clergy mingle with the representatives of the Buddhist, Hindu, and Sikh faiths. The atmosphere is one of co-operation. Sister Catherine, a contemplative nun of the Redemptrist order, is the guest speaker. Sister Catherine, aged about fifty, has put aside the nun's habit and dressed in tailored slacks and cashmere sweater. A silver cross about her neck, and a severe hair style are the singular signs of her renunciation. She possesses a deep contemplative wisdom, together, with a strong philosophic mind. She has spent the last number of years involved in Buddhist dialogue in Asia. She recalls the silence of the great stone Buddha at Polonnaruwa, in Ceylon. A silence that had filled her with the startling evidence of the reality of the void as described in Buddhist Sutras.

After listening to Sister Catherine's talk, you tell me that if you had not been a Buddhist, if *karma* had not brought you to India, you could certainly have found comfort in the contemplative orders of the Christian Church. Sister Catherine embodies for you the Christian ideal which includes aspects of Buddhist wisdom. Thomas Merton believed that it was this blending of Buddhism that could leaven Christianity in the West. Like Thomas Merton, you too are a bridge between East and West. You have fulfilled a unique role in the development of Buddhism in the West. It was through your endeavours that the young lamas who had fled Tibet were housed in the Young Lamas Home School at Dalhousie, which you had established. It is through your constant inspiration that the Karmapa has made this historic visit to America. Now, you teach Western students the foundations of Buddhist practice.

In your approach to teaching Buddhism, you remember that most western students possess either a Christian or Jewish background. But despite this early conditioning, you never limited instruction in the Dharma to fit into comfortable categories. You explained that taking the Refuge in the Buddha is a total commitment, a single-minded path. You made clear too, the fact that Westerners practice the monastic path of Tibetan Buddhism. This practice goes far beyond the nominal faith of the average Tibetan who invokes the mantra of Chenrezi, and gives respect to the Karmapa. The Westerner practices the arduous foundation path, the cornerstone of the Tantric Path of the Four Sects of Tibetan Buddhism. This foundation path includes meditation upon Precious human birth, impermanence, karma, and suffering. Then comes the taking of the Refuge in the Buddha...the engendering of compassion, prostrations, the practice of Vajra Sattva Purification meditation, and guru yoga.

I recall Tantric images, seen in pictures, engraved upon the rocks of Tibet; red stained outlines of the Vajra Yogini; dark forms of Padmasambhava; and the immaculate white Chenrezi. All ancient forms that are still symbols of the psychic renewal of man. All move me to an understanding of the insubstantiality of the world.

We drive up to Kinmount, a country meditation centre. We pass through Fennelon Falls, having left behind us the wintry landscape of Toronto. On the journey, you speak of the conversion of Yasa, a rich young man who had encountered the Buddha in the Deer Park. Upon hearing the Discourse of the Blessed one, the immaculate and stainless mind arose in him. Yasa immediately begged the Buddha to allow him to make the renunciation. This acceptance of Yasa by the Blessed one was the first formal ordination. It was only after the Fourth Buddhist Council in Ceylon, about 80 B.C., that the teachings of the Buddha were collected in the *Tripitaka*. The *Vinaya*, the disciplinary rules of conduct for the *Sangha*, were later committed to writing. During the Buddha's lifetime, the communities of monks and nuns were well established. Such a ripening has occurred in three Western women about to be ordained as nuns at Kinmount. Sister Palmo, the perfect *bikshuni*, you are anxious to witness the ceremony.

The ordination Ceremony is conducted privately in the Shrine Room presided over by the Karmapa and attended by only the monks and yourself. After the ceremony the new nuns emerge. They stand awkward in the winter sunlight, shifting new robes about their bodies, and feeling with frozen fingers their newly shaved heads. Later, in the cabin you share with an elderly nun:

"The requisite for a Buddhist nun is not necessarily a mastery of meditation. It is rather an ability to live a special kind of life. A woman who wishes to become a nun should examine her motive carefully. She should be able to live alone, no longer desire men, and abstain from alcohol. The vocation of a nun is more "dependent upon a lifestyle than control of the mind."

Anna, a newly ordained nun impresses me. She is a nurse by profession, and already in her late forties. She tells me that she had visited Cape Town, trying to be a settler there, close to a married daughter. The atmosphere of racial tension and that strange society had not been able to accommodate her. Driven by a spiritual need, she had visited India and come to see the ashram of Swami Muktananda. Here, the Karmapa was paying a courtesy visit. Seeing the Karmapa, and receiving his *darshan*, she understood that her quest was over. The Karmapa accepted her, and advised her to take further teachings. Two years later she had travelled to Kinmount for her ordination as a nun.

Sister Palmo, you are a Mother in Dharma. You are a help to the new nuns in a hundred different ways. You advise on the cutting

of robes; the rules of conduct; and meditation practice. You repeat
the injunction given by the Blessed One, one Century earlier:

"Go forth, monks, and teach the truth which is glorious in the
beginning, the middle, and the end for the good of all beings.
There are some whose eyes are not obscured by dust. Teach them,
they will understand."

At Kinmount, I sit a moment with you. I try and explain what
it has meant for me, both meeting and travelling with you. You
sense the question that shyness prevents me from asking:

"What people experience in meditation is not attributed to the
powers of the guru. Bliss and radiance occur of themselves when
the mind is tranquil. They are elements within the mind of the
meditator."

I wait in silence beside you, happy to be in the presence that inspires
such warmth and contains the hidden elements of wisdom.

Our journey next day, is through the darkness of a Canadian
November evening. The monks, together with us, chant the
Mahakala *puja*. I listen to the praises of these protective deities.
The Mahakalas usually ride a mule. They carry a bag of poison,
hanging from their saddle bags, which kills the enemies of the
teachings. They possess, too, a mirror of judgment, snake lasso,
and bow and arrows. The Mahakalas remove all obstacles to the
growth and practice of Dharma.

Beyond the window of the Combi, I sense the landscape and
trees. Further across oceans and continents lies Africa. The
Karmapa, the monks, and yourself leave soon for Samye Ling in

Scotland. I shall lose you soon. I must return to Africa, where my daughter in a boarding school patiently waits my return. My responsibilities crowd in. These few days have seen me severed from my ordinary life. For a brief spell I have fallen within the mandala of the Karmapa.

There is a final initiation at Bodhisattva House in Toronto. In the crowded shrine room, I find a place behind the newly ordained nun, Anna. The seductive pealing of the bell and the eloquent *mudra*s of the Karmapa fail to distract my attention from small scars on the head of the new nun. I recall how Anna had been shaved with the help of students at Kinmount. The harshness of life is symbolised in those small scars. Between the *mudra* of the Karmapa and Anna's scarred head, exists different worlds. Suffering and my desire for transcendence overwhelm me. I turn towards you, Sister Palmo. Yet your head is bowed in a total acceptance. You have gone beyond the rugged terrain of the dualities. You have reconciled the opposites. You do not put constructions upon such observations. You have awakened from the slumber of ignorance. All that arises in the mind is spontaneously pure.

That night I dream of you, Sister Palmo, in the form of the Vajra Yogini. You wear a crown of dried skulls and a necklace of severed heads. You carry a skull cup full of blood and a hooked knife. A trident leans against your shoulder. In the morning you give teachings. I sense the essence of the *yidam* in your own nature. You judge my progress. You understand my difficulties. You admit that the meditation text which I had been studying for three years is difficult. Yet you stress that the detailed visualisation of a deity, colours and ornaments, is there to exhaust the mind. It is a process similar to that used in the Zen teachings. After the mind is exhausted comes a blow from heaven. Realisation is often sudden.

Your departure is at hand. Sister Palmo, you are certain of our next meeting. It cannot be otherwise. Lady of Realisation, you are so certain of your powerful grasp upon life.

I had returned from America to my family in Africa. You, Sister Palmo, in contrast are travelling in the party of the Karmapa through the European winter of 1974. You are visiting the capital cities of Europe. In Rome, Pope Paul receives the Gyalwa Karmapa in private audience. You have a sense of the dialogue begun by Thomas Merton continuing in the presence of the Karmapa at St. Peters. From Denmark, you write of the enthusiasm of the hippie community for the lineage teachings. Marpa, the translator, and Milarepa, the poet and yogi, truly live for Scandinavian youth. From Amsterdam you write in answer to my letters that have followed you across Europe:

.....so many earthquaking and glorious things have happened and we are travelling on the good earth, and not in the sky. Glory be! Kosmos, and the Theosophical-Vedanta setting have made Holland interesting. Now we wait for the web of many colours called Paris. Dear, love and blessing of the Three Jewels. ....

Months pass on these travels. Later, Barbara writes that you have had a heavy bout of the flu. She has seen that you rest in the Paris Hilton Hotel. The crowds, the Northern winter, and the monotony of vegetarian food have taken their toll. You are no longer young, but a woman in the early sixties. Sister Palmo, you have always driven yourself hard in the service of others. Hearing this news of your fatigue, I am reminded of the weary letters of

Swami Vivekananda written at the turn of the century. A letter, written to Mary Hale, from Vivekananda, reflects the exhaustion that spiritual teachers surely suffer today:

...now I am longing for rest. Hope I will get some, and the Indian people will give me up. How I would like to become dumb for some years and not talk at all.

In May 1975, the long tour ends. You who have visited continents, witnessed foreign cities, and encountered thousands of faces in this grand cavalcade of Dharma, now go into a retreat. You write on arrival at Rumtek:

My retreat begins in a few days time, and there are piles of mail, things to study, to write. One month. The birds sing. We all feel happy to be home, and His Holiness is well. So am I. In the grace waves of the guru-lama....

You make your retreat upon the Chagchen Mahamudra. Your mind is understood as arising spontaneously - natural, free.

Two years pass before we meet again. You write from Rumtek Monastery and give news. The Indian Ocean, stretching between Africa and India, keeps us apart. Yet your presence is still felt in my world. From Rumtek you write:

His Holiness is well, and all's right with the world. Today one of our Incarnates, aged about 14, left for Ladakh and it was quite moving to see him leave the scene of his childhood. He will be trained to take charge of Kagydupa monks there.....

Travelling to Bombay in September, you write:

The first hint of Spring in this winter atmosphere. Everything is within the good black earth, and not even a hint of a shoot, green or otherwise shows the way to release...but in the refuge of the Triple Gem, we understand, our labours...

In November, writing again from Rumtek: (You also refer to the possibility of my joining you in California in 1976.)

.....the comforting feeling that we shall be able to meet in California next year...if that is in the stars and planets whirling in the great Cosmic Sky Mandala. Once his Holiness had an interview with a woman who had come by jet all the way from South America to see him. She had an impossibly difficult married life to an older man. His Holiness gave her one of his radiant smiles, and said: "When things are at their worst say, "Thanks to the Guru" and you will understand.

In February of the following year you had been on a visit to Nepal. You had again been a member of the Karmapa's party. The tour had been a special visit to the monastery where the Karmapa had given a series of high initiations. You wrote of this event:

His Holiness is a golden glowing Chenrezi Padmapani. Nepal was a saga of which I shall speak to you personally. The Monkey Temple at Swayambunath moves me more than Bodh Gaya which is old and wonderful too. The country of the Buddha; it has some transcendental quality of otherness and "nowness" too.

The extraordinary workings of karma does indeed bring me to California. My flight across the Poles is exhausting. Yet I am convinced that I must spend this time with you; live out the California Spring. You are the guru; the one who can impart the seed of Buddhahood. I recognise this fact. What had begun in the summer lit room in Cape Town five years ago will continue in the house in San Mateo.

I am again in your presence in America. Time has stood still. Sister Palmo, you fill the room with a great translucence. There is a terrible knowledge too. A heart ailment has been diagnosed. You are ill. I know this at first glance. The warmth of your embrace is drenched with a poignancy; a sense of time running out. There is no certainty that I shall find you again. Each morning I come to your room and receive a blessing. You are the embodiment of Tara, the Vajra Yogini, and the other deities of the mandala. I know no self consciousness in bowing before you.

At the Asian Institute, you give discourses. You reflect insights of your years of study, and also your own mystical experience of Burma. A woman *pandit*, you address jean-clad America. You discuss enlightenment and all its profound implications. You consider the psychological leap; the supreme logic; the brave *bodhisattva*; all are elements of Buddhahood. You advise each student to meditate for himself. Certain realisations are the fruit of intuition.

Despite a heavy schedule of interviews and lectures, you always preside at the luncheon table. You possess the palate of a yogi - demanding, changeable, and subtle. Sometimes you desire a spare vegetable dish. Another time, it is pork chops or shrimps. Visitors come to lunch - Alan Ginsberg, Claudio Naranjo, and Buddhist scholar, Stephen Beyer. You talk of philosophy, family life, and culture. You are a good listener, yet, you seldom laugh. Your insights into impermanence and death have not lead you to the "joking" realisations of the Zen Masters. Perhaps this is because you are also an Englishwoman of an earlier and more conservative generation. After lunch you rest in the garden, peaceful among the blue jays and flowering shrubs.

There are many accomplished woman yogis in the history of the Vajrayana. Tibetan Buddhism abounds in female deities, *dakinis,* and consorts of Buddhas and *bodhisattvas.* This feminine energy represents the principle of openness and a cutting through the confusion of mind. Historically too, the woman yogi is of great importance. Niguma, who lived in the eleventh century, was an accomplished woman siddha. She was in early life the wife of the Mahasiddha Naropa, who later renounced the householder's life and became a monk. Niguma, too, followed the path of Renunciation. She mastered Tantric teachings, and became renowned for her magical attainments. With this background, of a long tradition of woman siddhas, and yogis, it did not seem incongruous that, Sister Palmo, you bestow an inner initiation of the Kagyu lineage.

The text of the initiation speaks of the *samsaric* nature of existence and the skilful means to transcend suffering. As the Vajra Master, you welcome us into the mandala and crown each of us as your equals in Dharma. At this stage of the initiation, which deals with purification, you hand us two reeds of *kusa* grass. You explain your reason for this:

"Put the long reed under your body, and the short one beneath the pillow when you sleep tonight. The power of the initiation will cause dreams of a symbolic nature to occur."

Following your instructions, I place the reeds in the manner in which you suggested, on retiring. I immediately fall into a deep sleep and experience three different dreams. In the morning, I encounter you in your room, maroon clad in the robe of the bhikshuni. I explain the first dream; how I had simply found myself in an ancient Indian temple garden, a place of perfect peace. You merely nod and are silent about this dream. The second dream had been more in the nature of a nightmare, which I recount:

"There was a terrible weight, a dark figure upon my chest, crushing life out of my body. It was both terrifying and threatening...."

You interrupt my recounting of the nightmare and remark:

"The dark figure symbolises purification. This is not an uncommon dream. It is a good sign of impurity coming away. Think of delusion leaving you forever. Ignorance and fear cannot sway you again."

The third dream is more difficult to recount, for it involves you, Sister Palmo, appearing in an inner form.

"In the third dream, I am witness in Africa to terrible battles and turmoil. You, Sister Palmo, appear in the form of a white *yogini*. You wear a white robe and possess upstanding hair. Your visage is fearful. You wear a necklace of skulls about your neck and brandish a trident. You pacify the hordes of darkness."

I did not know it then, but when I returned to Africa, all the unleashed violence of the Soweto riots had broken out. You admit that the vision of the white *yogini* is yourself but in an inner form. You are silent about this emanation of your mystical presence in my dream. There are aspects of the yogi about you that manifest in extraordinary ways. You have a power to emanate and teach on inner levels. You are without doubt an accomplished *yogi* in the long tradition of woman *siddhas* going back to the all powerful saint, Niguma.

Sakyamuni Buddha, in his earthly life, studied medicine in the forests of India. Tibetan Buddhism has elaborated further and transformed him into a blue celestial Buddha of Medicine, Sangyes Menla, who appears in a lapis lazuli colour, and wears the three Dharma robes. He holds in his hand the Trimphala Amla fruit.

Sister Palmo, you too possessed an insight into healing. You had encouraged the nuns at the Tilokpur Monastery to learn the preparation of herbal remedies under the instruction of a lama. Often, you could sense an illness either physical or psychological in a student and suggest a remedy. You always advocate that healing is a full time study and occupation. You encourage students to pray to Sangyes Menla, the Buddha of Medicine. At San Mateo, you perform a special healing Buddha Puja and distribute blessed pills to the sick.

Later in the garden, you talk with elderly Major and Mrs. Knight. You speak about Dharamsala and the presence of the Dalai Lama, whom you honour and revere. Major and Mrs. Knight have lived many years in India, and have given support to exiled lamas. You did not realise it then, that only a week later, Major Knight would die of a heart attack. When you heard this news later at the breakfast table you said:

"It is no great sadness to die in old age. Easier to leave life in good health. Why suffer, if when *karma* is worked out, the thread of life snaps. Major Knight had lead a good life. We cannot shun the inevitable. Death comes to all."

You take up the vigil beside Major Knight's body. You conduct the *Phowa* prayers. The aggregates that had left the physical body now make the journey to the *bardo* realm. You console Mrs. Knight. Your vigil beside the body is of a classical simplicity. I recall your visit to South Africa, when you had been called upon to perform the Buddhist funeral prayers at the cremation of a Chinese seaman who had been murdered in a dockside brawl over a prostitute. You had seen beyond the sordid aspects of the man's death, and rather perceived his radiant essence. An extraordinary woman from India, Sister Palmo, you had come to Africa in order to guide a seaman through the realms of the *bardo* night. Africa and Asia met in you in an unusual interweaving. Now, you are linked with Major Knight, and again perform the ancient rite for the newly dead.

During this memorable week, you talk to an enclosed order of Carmelite nuns. The nuns are dark shapes, behind grilles, who listen intently to your lecture. You speak about Buddhist meditation, and life at Rumtek Monastery. You explain how Buddhists meditate alone in a cell. This had been the method in Tibet, when yogis had inhabited caves, and monks have sought out isolated hermitages. Buddhists like Christians come together for prayers or as in the case of Buddhists, for the celebration of puja. Yet, I know from my discussion with you that the Buddhist sects have in their discipline rich aspects of yoga. It is the energy of passion, transmuted and controlled, that forms the basis of realisation. Such insights are surely not intrusive upon these women, Carmelite nuns, dedicated, like yourself, to a life of the spirit.

In California, you spoke often of Trungpa Rinpoche. As a youth, Trungpa had come to your home in India together with Akong Rinpoche. Both lamas had begged your assistance. Like a mother, you took them as sons into your own home. Later, you arranged for a scholarship to Oxford for the young Trungpa. In those early years, Trungpa had possessed a radiant purity. But now you understand that the Lama had taken on Western karma, and taught in the manner of a *siddhic* teacher. The Karmapa on his visit had called Trungpa Rinpoche the Padmasambhava of the West.

Trungpa Rinpoche, dignified in a tailored suit, receives you in a house in Berkeley. The lama greets you in a formal fashion - the head blessing customary between a guru and disciple. You had brought a text of a Mahamudra translation for the Rinpoche's comments. Conversation is between old friends. The Lama speaks of the coming visit to the Karmapa to America in the winter. He talks too of his own intention to make a yearlong retreat.

Trungpa Rinpoche sees in you, Sister Palmo, the generous woman who had helped him in India. He senses too the depth of the yogi within you. He had helped to bring these powers to fruition. The Rinpoche recalls that he had not dared give the Phowa teachings for fear that you might not have returned to your body. He recognised the exquisite delicacy of your insights; the deftness of your manipulation of the veins and the airs of the Six Yogas of Naropa.

On this afternoon in Berkeley, the Rinpoche is totally at ease; the links between you both span fifteen years. You possess the same Vajra energy and an integrity that makes the efforts of ordinary people seem strained in comparison.

Later, when I had returned to Africa, Barbara writes that Trungpa Rinpoche had come to bless the Shrine Room at San Mateo. On this occasion, the lama had changed the lineage prayers of Karma Pakshi. Sister Palmo, you had knelt in contemplation in the shrine room. The Rinpoche had turned to you and remarked:

"I shall not see you again. But after the passing of time, we shall be reunited."

A look of compassion shadowed Trungpa Rinpoche's face as if he had a premonition of your passing.

From Africa, I had written earlier in the year requesting the Green Tara Initiation from your hands. Here, in the California Spring, you confer this empowerment, the authority to meditate upon the green and lovely form of Tara.

During the initiation, you instruct me not to see your physical aspect as a Buddhist nun, the composed woman of sixty-five, but I must instead concentrate upon you in the form of Green Tara, a sixteen year old virgin girl, bejewelled, and blossoming in youthful vigour.

I enter the shrine room, and prostrate before you. The altar is piled high with offerings, flaming candles, and an image of the Buddha. I see you in the form of the radiant Goddess, Green Tara.

Before you bestow the initiation, you say:

"Every teacher, before giving an empowerment must speak of their authority and competence to do so. I have heard His Holiness, the Dalai Lama, speak very humbly of his own attainment before a great initiation that he was about to have given in India. The Dalai Lama was humble and modest as is any great lama. It is hard for me, with this in mind, to present my own accomplishments. Simply believe that I have the authority, and the ability, to bestow this initiation."

The reformer, Atisha, and Marpa, the translator, are among the ancient lineage holders of this initiation which has come down through the line of Karmapa Lamas. As the ceremony progresses, you finally place the *torma* of initiation upon my head. At that moment, I see myself as the embodiment of Green Tara; she is both a reflection of yourself, and the deity beyond. This insight is one of the deep mysteries of Tibetan Buddhism, the knowledge that Tara is both a creation of mind and a real deity.

In the Shrine Room, I meditate upon the beauty of this peaceful empowerment. Tara's tranquillity is about your presence, Sister Palmo. It suffuses the Shrine Room and makes those who have received the initiation aware of a centre of peace within their own hearts. Yet, even at this moment, I sense the poignancy. I must leave you again. I no longer have the certainty of finding you once more. Your life energy is diminishing.

Shortly before I leave, you receive me formally in the sitting room. In the robe of the Mahayana nun, you indicate the territory of *shunyata*, which the meditator will encounter in practice.

"The experience of shunyata shakes the foundation of one's being. But you must not despair. For a period, emptiness in the sense of living in a world without concepts, name and form, overtakes one. There is a sense of total aloneness, even meaninglessness.

Students suffer intensely. Yet, it is essential to the path. All the practice of meditation upon form, *sadhana*, and empowerments lead only to this realisation. If we do not experience *shunyata* then all the teachings of the Buddha remain dry discourses."

I listen intently. I recall your experience in Burma; the warning given by the Thai monk; the vision of the lotus upon the sea; how your life was irrevocably altered.

You continue to speak about the problems inherent in the practice of meditation:

"Meditation is never easy. Even with myself it has been hard. Babajie allowed me simply to remain at home when as a lay woman I felt shattered, or unable to take upon the practicalities of daily life. Meditation means coming to terms with one's own energies."

I sense the rightness of your insight, and know from my own fragmented self just how delicate the energies of the subtler realms are.

"Recently, I received empowerments from His Holiness the Dalai Lama that had left me withdrawn. I felt removed from life. His Holiness Karmapa encouraged me rather to return to daily activities and give up on the long hours of sitting practice. He urged me to practice Mahamudra, the awareness of life itself. You will discover this for yourself along the path."

This last profound advice is the final instruction that you give me. In retrospect, the essence remains. Now with you gone, this injunction still sustains me.

It is fitting that on the evening of my departure, Barbara plans a program of Tibetan music and chanting. Sensing my departure, I feel the need to pay a special tribute to you. Barbara and I find the original Gelongma Palmo text which you had translated into English. This ancient teaching tells of Gelongma Palmo, a woman saint of remarkable *siddhic* powers, dwelling in the forest hermitages of India. Barbara and I read this tribute to you, Sister Palmo, before the presentation of Tibetan music in the Shrine Room, "The biography of the original Gelongma Palmo (known in Sanskrit as the Bhikshuni Srimati) who lived in the eighth century in India still exists."

"One should imagine the form of a woman with the yellow robe who lived in a hermitage, following the path of the yogi, dwelling in a forest, living a life of seclusion and meditation. We should not forget the powerful energies of Buddhism of that period. This was the time of the great Nalanda University, and the writings of the sublime poetry of Shantideva.

The biography tells us in its spare fashion that the Gelongma Palmo showed herself in her outer form as the Bhikshuni, wearing the yellow Dharma robe, with an *ushnisha* mound upon her head, like the Buddha.

In her inner form, she manifested as Tara in green colour, removing all obstacles and hindrances. Meditation on Gelongma Palmo in this form, we should recollect the very beautiful initiation of the Green Tara which we experienced this morning.

In her secret form, the Gelongma Palmo appeared as a *siddha*, one who possesses miraculous powers. The story tells us that she appeared in the form of a *siddha*, cutting off her head, and put it on the trident of Guru Padmasambhava.

It is enough to see the Gelongma Palmo as one who had embodied a triple identity - the outer form of the woman in the yellow robe, the nun who had taken the renunciation, the inner form as an emanation of Green Tara, and the secret form of the *siddha*, the one of magical attainment.

The Gelongma Palmo reached the Tenth stage of the Bodhisattvas when "the simultaneously arising of the mind" occurred, in its nature very pure. The understanding of the *Dharmakaya* is clear. The nature of thoughts are utterly pure, clear and transparent. The Gelongma Palmo possessed the *Sambhogakaya* body of celestial bliss.

All this happened in the heart centre of Bodh Gaya centuries ago, and where pilgrims still flock to the holy places of the Buddha."

You, Sister Palmo, of the twentieth century are moved at our insights. You are indeed an emanation of the ancient *siddha*, Gelongma Palmo, who dwelt in the forests of India. I follow the reading of the biography of the original Gelongma Palmo, with your translation of her outpouring of praises, the hymn to the bodhisattva, Chenrezi.

"The following lyric hymn to Chenrezi was composed by the original Gelongma Palmo as an outpouring of praise. What is the nature of such praise? We have to retrace our steps back in time to those who understood such an outpouring of the heart - Rumi, the great Sufi poet and sage, and St. John of the Cross ..."

Om, Protector of the Universe, I bow down.

Praise him, lama of the Universe and the Three Spheres,

Praise him, the King of the Gods and Mara and Brahma

Praised by the Sakyamuni, supreme among Jinas,
giver of realisations.

You, sister Palmo, listen to the rendering of the hymn to Chenrezi. It reflects the outpouring of your own great heart. You too aspire to the ecstasy of St. John of the Cross, the heightened bliss of the Sufi poets. All this joy overflows from the hymn to Chenrezi, the glorious bodhisattva of compassion. As if an echo to all this a bearded youth chants, with a deep resonance of sound, the Mani mantra. You acknowledge our tribute to you with a wordless recognition. We have penetrated your heart's essence.

Next morning, before my departure, you receive me. You are simply Sister Palmo, the woman who has taken the ordination and wears the robe of the nun. You are formal, and place a traditional white scarf about my neck, and bestow the "head blessing," a bond shared between guru and disciple. The warmth of your brow amazes. How can I ever doubt that this life energy might cease! Then I leave your presence for the last time.

On my return to Africa, I am moved by Barbara's letters from Mount Shasta, which describes a retreat you made on the slopes of that ancient mount, revered by the American Indian. Here at the foot of Mountain Shasta, a non active volcano, 14,000 feet high, you completed a two week retreat. Attended by Barbara, and your Tibetan nun, Pema Zangmo, you spend the days in meditation. The cry of coyotes, changing winds, and the gusting of trees does not disturb. The mind remains natural, beyond the dualities. The territory of formless Mahamudra meditation.

Sister Palmo, you emerge from the retreat with a radiance. You possess the mien of a wise and powerful deity. You have achieved an insight which is far from empirical thought. A deeply intuitive insight of the unity of nature, and the acceptance of impermanence and death.

Returning to San Mateo, you celebrate the tenth anniversary of your ordination as a Buddhist Nun. A decade earlier, you had on ordination adopted the name Karma Khechog Palmo. You wore the maroon robe of the Bhikshuni for the first time. You went about shaven headed. With a fierce devotional energy, you had worked for the welfare of Lamas, and the bringing of Tibetan Buddhism to the West. Now, in the garden at San Mateo, you look back on those eventful years. Many come to the anniversary celebrations. Musicians play in the garden. There is an anniversary cake with ten burning candles, one for each year of your saga as a nun. Old friends in America, new young students, Allen Ginsberg, and Lama Karma Thinley, of Toronto, come to wish you well and great happiness. I, who are far from you that day, send you a letter in which I try and speak of the meaning of your ordination to me in my own life:

My Dear Mummy:

I would wish very much to be in your presence during the celebration of your Renunciation. As this is not possible, I shall simply meditate at my own shrine.

In my own life, I see with clarity the three poisons - greed, ignorance and hatred, the feelings which sway both the mind and the emotions. The only release is to cease from suffering in the manner in which the Buddha discovered it for all. The natural outcome of such thoughts is the taking of the Renunciation or the Going Forth. Surely, the Renunciation is not only the relinquishing of attachment and craving, but also the reaching out towards a greater compassion and emotional maturity.

In reading the life of the Buddha, I find again and again this phrase. Here it is repeated as when Yasa, the young man, said to the Buddha: "Lord, I wish to receive the going forth and the Full Admission of the Blessed one." "Come Bhikku," the Blessed one said: "The Law is well proclaimed. Lead the holy life for the complete end of suffering."

This is the great simplicity, which is found, when all else has been exhausted.

When the Blessed one spoke to Yasa, and others, the phrase repeatedly recurs:

"...the spotless, immaculate vision of the Dhamma rose up in him."

I wonder what is meant by that immaculate vision of the Dhamma. Is it the thought that urges one to enlightenment? Is it the essence of bodhicitta, the Buddha nature? These are words that suggest complex intellectual stirrings. But in essence, I think that the "spotless, immaculate vision" does not refer to a vision of life that is purely intellectual. Rather, it is an innate understanding of original mind, the radiant void.

These are my thoughts on this day of your perfect Renunciation. There is nothing material that I can offer since all material things are exhausted and subject to change...

My letter does reach you on that anniversary day in California. Your reply, Sister Palmo, arrives some weeks later. You continue on your journey - first to New York, and then make an unexpected trip to your son, Kabir, who is filming in South America. After this detour, you cross the Atlantic for a brief two days in London. Finally, when you do return to India, in September, you write from Calcutta:

....your beautiful anniversary letter, and the poem that is deep and meaningful, as well as the book, "The Life of the Buddha".....just the cool water of Dharma, I was looking for....reached me. All treasures. This is the true meaning of His Holiness Karmapa' Guruji's stress on Triyana Dharmachakra. Without the Golden Buddha and the sutras, the very foundation of Tibetan Buddhism is missing.

I am truly happy that you have found it all....and I know in my heart that this is a sign for you one day, hopefully in this life itself, there will be a Rabjung or Going Forth, when your family responsibilities are fulfilled....

Your letter was something that I could hardly bear to read. I am a woman with a family and a vocation. But that you should have considered me worthy of such a revolutionary step, as the ordination of a Buddhist nun, moved me to tears. Rather, I now think of this progression in a future life time. The present, the power and beauty of the world still summons me. Significant therefore, that this knowledge of an aspect of my own nature had to come miraculously from your intuitive insight. I would never have had the courage to speak about any of this directly to you.

There comes a day when I am far from you. I am sitting in meditation before my shrine. You are in retreat in Rumtek Monastery. Yet, I sense your presence, the warmth of your hands upon my head, the joy of your smile. Quite suddenly, I see it. Realise that this quality has always been there. It is the innate purity of my own mind, the radiant void that is without beginning or end. The first glimpse of *Mahamudra*, the naked awareness of mind itself. A verse of meditation, which you had translated returns to me:

"As the Great River flows on

Whatever meditation sitting you do silently

This then is always the Buddha's nature enlightenment

The world just isn't there

And all this is the great Bliss."

You, Sister Palmo, have always known this. Your mind is the effortless mind of the state of Mahamudra.

Sister Palmo, you died on the 28th of March, 1977. Pema Zangmo, your attendant nun, wrote on that last day of your life. It was no different to any other day that you had crowded with love and care:

...now I would like to tell something about our late Mummy. Before the death of Mummy - that is about 6 p.m. - there was a Tibetan Friendship Group Conference. AL that time she had no trouble or illness at all. There were many people from different countries there. They had a grand feast, and our late Mummy gave a speech. After the conference, we went for a walk to see her relatives. Moreover she gave advice to many devoted disciples.

After a few hours, we had a short rest, and I went to see her. I thought she was sleeping. But unfortunately, she had gone forever, leaving me behind. There were many good signs on that day. She passed away in the meditation pose, her face tangled by rainbows. A light rain was falling outside. Everybody was surprised at the auspicious signs rare for this time of the year. Many spoke that they were blessed to have see you - the holy one....

Sister Palmo, your death was peaceful. By the manner in which you departed, in the meditation pose, you defeated the terror of death. You had escaped by the power of yoga, through the *brahmananda*, the exit of the *yogi's*, at the crown of the head. Only your physical body journeys to the cremation ground. You are dressed in the maroon robe of the Mahayana nun and flowers surround your body. Your sons kneel and weep joyfully. Numerous rainbows are seen in the sky. Many high lamas chant prayers in order to reconcile your essence in the *bardo* world. Kabir, your son, and Pema Zangmo take your ashes to Rumtek monastery. What is left of your physical body is returned to its rightful place. What is of the essence, the spirit, lingers in the Clear Light Void.

Though death had manifested itself in you, my beliefs are not shattered. Rather, I see the wisdom in becoming reconciled to impermanence and suffering. These are the basic tenants of Buddhist thought. Sister Palmo, you were as much a bundle of flesh and tendencies as myself. I grieve for you, but only out of my own loss of your presence in my life.

Yet, by virtue of your Bodhisattva Vow, you must return to Samsara in order to work unremittingly for the sake of all sentient beings. You embody too much of the nature of Green Tara, the female bodhisattva, to abandon re-birth and seek a high place in the *Sukhavati* Heaven. On the forty-ninth day of the *bardo* period, you will incarnate in a new body. Your essence will again touch the living. Yet, I will not see you again, Sister Palmo, in this life. The experience was lived out. The texts which you had translated continue to inspire. I travel the path of Dharma which you opened.

Since your death, I have had three consecutive dreams. In these dreams you appear in repose. You are dressed in the robes of the Mahayana nun. In your right hand, you hold a bunch of golden hanging fruit. You speak the words:

"This is the teaching. This is all there is to understand."

The Koan which you gave is the jewel of the Tibetan teaching; the realisation that *Samsara* and *Nirvana* are in essence one. An understanding that goes beyond any formal sitting practice. Sister Palmo you passed through the "gateless gate" on the journey of "there being no path to traverse." The world simply is, and your presence allows life to flow on.

GLOSSARY

AMITABHA BUDDHA: The buddha of boundless light, and discriminating wisdom.

AVALOKITESVARA: The compassionate bodhisattva of mercy.

BARDO: Intermediary period between death and rebirth.

BIKSHUNI: A fully ordained Buddhist nun.

BODHICHITTA: The seed of enlightenment.

BODHISATTVA: One without ego, who works for the liberation of all sentient beings.

BODHISATTVA VOW: A promise to save all sentient beings.

DHARMA: Teachings of the Buddha.

DHARMAKAYA: The Logos. The primordial ground of all appearance understood as shunyata, or emptiness.

GAMPOPA: Lineage teacher of the Kagyu sect. A pupil of Milarepa, the yogi poet. A renowned scholar and founder of the Kagyu tradition and the Karmapa lineage.

GELONGMA: An ordination which gives a nun the same status as that of a monk. The gelongman ordination comes through a line of Zen teachings.

HINAYANA: The Lesser Vehicle. The orthodox form of Buddhism as established after the life time of the Budda. The Hinayana claims never to have left the true doctrine, which is set forth in the Pali canon.

KAGYU LINEAGE: The sect of Tibetan Buddhism founded by Marpa, the translator, in the eleventh century. This tradition emphasises the oral or "ear whispered" transmission.

KARMA GATHERERS: One who naturally can help others by their own actions.

MAHAMUDRA: Also known as "the great seal." The understanding of the nature of the mind.

MAHAYANA:The Greater Vehicle, the schools of Buddhism that followed the reform of the Hinayana between 100 A.D and 200 A.D. The Mahayana embodies the bodhisattva ideal as well the realisation of emptiness, or voidness. Its doctrines derive from the Sanskrit version of the Buddhist canon.

NIRMANAKAYA: The historical Gautama Buddha is a manifestation of the Nirmanakya, an earthly form of the Buddha.

NIRVANA: The state of enlightenment.

NYINGMAPA TRADITION: The original sect of Tibetan Buddhism founded by Padmasambhava.

PADMASAMBHAVA: The founder of Tibetan Buddhism in Tibet in the middle of the eighth century. He established the Nyingma tradition known as the ancient ones.

PHOWA: Tibetan rituals and prayers for the dying.

PRATYEKBUDDHA: One who meditates to achieve enlightenment for himself alone.

SAMATHA MEDITATION: The development of "one pointedness" of mind. A concentrated and calm state.

SAMADHI: One pointed meditation free from all clinging to experience and sensory perception.

SAMBHOGAKAYA: A blissful form of Buddha activity pertaining to the bodhisattvas, which inspire devotees to strive for Buddhahood.

SAMSARA: The state of suffering.

SHUNYATA: The empty nature of the mind. Also known as the void.

TANTRA: A spiritual system of practices, used for gaining enlightenment.

TARA: A compassionate female goddess known generally in a green or white form.

VAJRAYANA: The school of Tibetan buddhist teachings. It is also known as the adamantine way, the short path to enlightenment.

VAJRAYOGINI: An important and fierce female deity of the Kagyu tradition.

VIPASSANA MEDITATION: The practice of insight, the quality of examination of the mind.

Sheila Fugard is a South African novelist and poet. She is the author of three novels, *The Castaways, Rite of Passage,* and *A Revolutionary Woman.* She has also published four volumes of poetry. She lives in Southern California and has been a Tibetan Buddhist since the early seventies. www.sheilafugard.com